T0356277

Praise for *Grace Yourself*

"Chris Janssen walks us through the complexities and confusion surrounding addiction and growth and recovery with grace, humility, patience, and honesty. She also brings wisdom that has ancient roots and is research informed. This is a compelling invitation to sobriety at its best and most joyful."

—**JOHN ORTBERG,** Founder of Become New and
Author of *Steps: A Guide to Transforming Your Life
When Willpower Isn't Enough*

"No matter what has left you feeling powerless—alcohol, food, exercise, substances—Chris Janssen's *Grace Yourself* will help you regain your power. Through her own remarkably honest personal story combined with her wisdom gained through her work as a life coach, Chris guides the reader through the psychology of addiction to change what you might believe and help you rewrite your story. Whether you are struggling with unhealthy lifestyle choices or know someone who is, this book is a must-read for anyone wanting to understand themselves or those they love. Filled with exercises, information, and reflection, it is a transformational read that should be on everyone's list."

—**KATHY IZARD,** Author of *Trust the Whisper,
The Hundred Story Home,* and *The Last Ordinary Hour*

"Life is a messy mix of beauty and chaos simultaneously. I believe in showing up at work, home, and in community as the same person. With a recent choice to live alcohol-free after years of unknowingly using my own vices to cope with overwhelm, stress, and daily struggles, I believe this is a book everyone should read. In *Grace Yourself,* Chris Janssen shares stories and lessons from her personal and professional lives, blending her pains and celebrations with her coaching tools. With relatability and actionable takeaways, this book will highlight the purpose in all the things that make you, *you*! It is a necessary reminder that every chapter in your story is worthy and has purpose!"

—**AJ VADEN,** CEO and Cofounder of
Brand Builders Group and Cohost of
The Influential Personal Brand Podcast

"There are so many meaningful and introspective takeaways from Chris Janssen's book. No matter what you may be working through and striving to overcome, this book will guide you through it by providing key messages and tools to bolster self-worth and inspire the innate desire to grow and evolve. It's never too late to make a change in your life, and Chris's personal story— along with her selflessness in giving back—is an incredible road map for doing just that."

—**EMILY BLAIR MARCUS,** Founder and CEO
of Emily Blair Media

"*Grace Yourself* is full of truths that free those trapped by addiction from the lies they've been told. In a journey that often feels isolating, Chris shares her personal story like a trusted friend with the wisdom of an accomplished coach. This book empowers readers to know their worth, shift their mindset, and change their lives."

—**DOUG MILLER,** Lead Pastor of Plum Creek Church
in Castle Rock, Colorado

"*Grace Yourself* is a piece of hope for anyone stuck in an addictive cycle or close to someone who is suffering. The book offers compassionate insights combined with practical tools to empower readers to embrace their value. With true empathy and wisdom, Chris Janssen gives a compelling insight to the complexities and realities of recovery, giving readers the comforting realisation that healing is difficult but possible! I would recommend this book to anyone who is affected either directly or indirectly with addiction/negative cycles."

—**CHERRY BEAGLES,** CEO & Founder of The 400 Club, London

"If you want freedom from harmful habits or controlling thoughts, *Grace Yourself* will get you unstuck! This book shines light on addiction's effects on driven achievers and high performers. It is also a bold reminder of the worth and resourcefulness we all possess, and how we can find grace in our path toward healing."

—**JACEK WALISZEWSKI,** Award-winning Author and US Army Special Forces Green Beret

"No matter where you've been, what you've done, or whether you are stuck in an addictive pattern or not, you are worthy of love and belonging. In *Grace Yourself*, Chris Janssen writes like a trusted friend, reminding you that grace can't be earned, change is possible, and you already have everything you need to move toward the life you want."

—**ASHLEY EICHER,** Founder and CEO of AE Entertainment

"She's done it again! Chris has opened the window of her journey towards sobriety and challenged us to go deeper into our own journeys with her to a place of freedom and grace. Chris does this with vulnerability to her learnings and gives us practical ways that draw us into places we want to go but lack the skill or courage to go alone. Read at the risk of discovery and freedom. Go ahead... grace yourself!"

—**STEVE CLIFFORD,** Pastor Emeritus of Westgate Church in Silicon Valley and Founding Board Member of Transforming the Bay with Christ

"Whether you are seeking release from an addiction, controlling thoughts, perfectionism, or just want to move forward, *Grace Yourself* will help! Written with kindness and conviction, this book provides tools for getting unstuck while reminding you of the worthiness you already possess."

—**AVIJAH SCARBROUGH,** Journalist, Lifestyle Reporter, Producer, and TV Host of *Good Morning Vail*

"Upon reading *Grace Yourself* I was profoundly moved. Chris Janssen's brave act in writing this book unlocked memories of my father precisely because the author revealed what I wish my own father could have received with the grace presented here. Having lost a parent to alcoholism, I have struggled with inevitable questions that arose as a survivor of an alcoholic who could not overcome their impulses, anxiety, and self-doubt. As a result, I have been keenly attuned to messages throughout my adult life that might help answer my own questions of purpose and self-awareness to help guide my conversations with my own child, my spouse, and my professional teams regarding anxiety, resentment, and the peace which follows from empathy—for others and for one's self.

At the core of *Grace Yourself* is a message about healing so that when people are speaking to you—as a parent, a friend, a spouse, a leader, or team member—their interaction can be received through a filter of compassion, acceptance, love, and self-respect instead of a filter of hurt, shame, and impulsiveness. The profound message I took from Chris Janssen's journey is that people see life through the lens of how they feel inside and that the power to change and build community is anchored in self-acceptance and an ability to seek community, ask for help, and be willing to pursue becoming the most healed and present version of yourself. The impact will be felt by generations to follow."

—**TIM SHEPHARD,** Vice President, Enterprise Strategy at Lockheed Martin Space

"Like grief, alcoholism and other addictions can harm how we see ourselves—our worth. Chris Janssen's vulnerability, written on every page, is just what you need to get through those tough times. Her experiences will help you with your past and encourage your future. I'm thankful to call Chris Janssen my friend."

—**THEO BOYD,** Author of *My Grief Is Not Like Yours*

Grace Yourself

—

**How to Show Up for
the Sober Life You Want**

Chris Janssen

Published by Mission Driven Press, an imprint of Forefront Books, Nashville, Tennessee.

Distributed by Simon & Schuster.

Library of Congress Control Number: 2024918863

Print ISBN: 978-1-63763-337-3
E-book ISBN: 978-1-63763-338-0

Cover Design by Studio Gearbox
Interior Design by Bill Kersey, KerseyGraphics

Printed in the United States of America

Dedication

For you and me.

Table of Contents

Part II
Discovery: What Happened

Part III
Recovery: What It's like Now

Note to
the Reader

*We can ignore even pleasure. But pain insists
upon being attended to. God whispers to us in our
pleasures, speaks in our conscience, but shouts in our
pains: it is His megaphone to rouse a deaf world.*[1]
—C. S. LEWIS

SOME OF US RECOVER LOUDLY—IN HOPES OF preventing others from dying quietly. This book is me being loud. As much as I may want to, I cannot choose sobriety for you. That is your decision. But I can help you show up for the sober life you deserve, should you choose it.

I am a board-certified coach with a master's degree in counseling psychology and have worked with hundreds of peak-performing athletes, singers, dancers, writers, artists, soldiers, entrepreneurs, and small businesses to close the gap between where they are and where they want to be. While my academic expertise is not addiction specific, I am an expert at my own recovery from alcohol addiction and am qualified to share my story with you. My sweet spot as a coach is in helping clients substitute limiting beliefs and unhelpful stories with certainty and narratives that serve them. The reason this is my inclination is that I had a lousy story in the past that narrated my self-worth, which led me to develop tools to change my beliefs about myself, my worth, my power, and my recovery. Now I get to share my experience, tools, and coach training with you, so you, too, can show up for the life you want.

People change when the pain of being the same becomes greater than the pain of changing.

If you're offered promises for an easy way to sobriety, it is your cue to get curious and ask questions. I've followed several such claims unsuccessfully. No amount of academic research, science, money, fancy rehabs, medicine, hypnotherapy, psilocybin therapy, yoga, or quick-fix literature will free you of your habit if you have not first chosen that freedom for yourself and are certain *why* freedom is a must for you. Those things, while potential supplements to recovery, are not substitutions for your personal commitment to it.

People change when the pain of being the same becomes greater than the pain of changing. Successful sobriety stories include some level of suffering. That level, sometimes referred to as "hitting bottom," is different for everyone. I've listened to thousands of recovery stories over the past eighteen years—no two have the identical circumstantial reasons to quit digging. The common denominator to people's continuous success is that they reached a level of pain that made change a must. One person's bottom may be the loss of their marriage, finances, legal rights, job, home, or freedom, while another person's bottom is the feeling of sadness. On the flip side, I've listened to people tell of horror after horror happening to them and still not reaching the limit of their pain threshold. Yes, people do get sober because of circumstances (a person who goes to jail is forced to get clean) or to quell the fear of a loved one. The question to ask in that case is, *Is that reason enough to* stay *sober?* Maybe, maybe not. I've learned that the pain, not the circumstance surrounding the pain, fuels sustainable change. Addiction will fight to take us out no matter what—until we decide we deserve to be free of it no matter what.

If you are stuck in an addictive snare and your soul is screaming *No more!*, you are ready to receive help. If you are looking for a temporary refuge from, or a healthy way to moderate, your habit, there are books and programs available to you. But if you want to live all in, alcohol-free, and show up for the life you deserve, keep reading. Together we've got this!

I embraced and enjoyed thirteen-plus years of continuous sobriety and the life that came with it. I thought I chose sobriety for me, yet I came to learn that I chose it for my family and out of fear of what-ifs. I chose it to hold it together. So at age fifty-two, after becoming an empty nester with less to hold together and with previous fears faded, I became drinking-curious. I love fun. What if I wasn't living my best life? What if there was even more fun and fulfillment to gain? I wondered, *Why can't I go for a life I love with an occasional drink? I must find out.*

I'm writing this book for anyone questioning whether to include or exclude a habit from their lives. Answering my own drinking-curious call after continuous freedom led me to uncover even more of myself, discover my reasons ("whys") I deserve to live free, and recover my sobriety. This is an *un*covery, *dis*covery, and *re*covery story.

As a coach, my goal is to help you uncover your blind spots, reveal your strengths, and partner with you to get unstuck. As such, in this book, I'll offer tools and exercises for you to process your own uncovery, discovery, and recovery. I want to help you tap into your own cleverness, curiosity, and resourcefulness to close the gap between where you are and where you want to be.

With love,
Chris

PART I

Uncovery: What It Was Like

Chapter 1

Magic

It is at the bottom where we find grace; for like water, grace seeks the lowest place and there it pools up.

—RICHARD ROHR

Y FIRST SIP OF ALCOHOL WAS MAGICAL. I WAS A freshman in high school, and my girlfriends and I loved being friends with upperclassmen who had driver's licenses and cars. We parked at a popular hangout spot in the foothills of Northern California, creating our own party on the side of a dirt road on a spring night. It wasn't magical because of the company I was with or the significance of the celebration. It wasn't magical because of any milestone or coming of age or any enjoyment that television commercials and marketing romanticize as a reward for drinking alcohol with friends. Alcohol was magical because of the way it made me feel—from the first sip.

Although I remember the surrounding situation vaguely, I remember my feeling in detail. I can't tell you exactly which friends I was with, which upperclassmen drove, or what the cars looked, smelled, or felt like. But I can tell you the first sip of alcohol, from a beer can, hit my tongue and went straight to my brain, igniting a sensation that all was well, calm, and right in my world. I felt OK. As a high-achieving perfectionist who rarely felt centered or satisfied, I felt content. It was enchanting.

The mystique faded as fast as it arrived during that freshman year, and I learned to detest alcohol—for the feelings that showed up *after* the first sip. The hangovers, the memory loss of the previous nights, and the guilt and remorse that accompanied mornings after drinking stuck me in a shame spiral that my friends and later Scott, my husband, did not seem to experience or understand. Still, from age fourteen to thirty-seven, I continued to drink alcohol socially throughout high school, college, graduate school, being a newlywed, and then as a new parent—never realizing that the euphoric first-sip feelings I experienced were not the same as other drinkers, or "normies," around me were feeling. *Normie* is a name used in some recovery communities for people able to drink a bit of alcohol without it igniting an unquenchable obsession for more.

I was successful at school, relationships, and my career. I did not exhibit signs that screamed "problem drinker" to those around me, such as drinking daily or before 5 p.m., getting a DUI, being arrested, or missing work or important events. I didn't drink during my pregnancies or while nursing. I lived for twenty-three years in my own conflicted head scheming ways I could quit alcohol forever—then rationalizing why it was no big deal to accomplish two things: satisfy my first-sip hit and blend into social norms. My body was addicted to a pattern of spiking dopamine, and my mind was addicted to the comfort of fitting in.

The rationalizing came easy to me. Placing unattainable standards on myself and then beating myself up for not reaching them came naturally. My pattern was to decide never, ever, *ever* to drink again; bump up against that first-sip craving; and then counsel myself to *chill out, take the sip, don't be a perfectionist. You don't have a problem with alcohol—otherwise, people would tell you so. You have a problem with oversensitivity, overthinking, and being too hard on yourself. People have told you so. You're going to ostracize yourself. Relax. Be normal and take the sip.* Thus, the cycle—of craving . . . sip . . . obsession for more sips . . . hangover . . . guilt . . . shame . . . remorse . . . never again—would continue swirling.

Guilt is thinking you did something wrong. Shame is thinking you're a bad person. I had both. Setting nearly impossible goals for myself set me up for believing I was wrong on the occasions I did not reach them—guilt. Linking my worth to my actions set me up for believing I was a bad person on the occasions I did not meet my high standards—shame. If you relate to this, know that you are worthy regardless of your actions, and there is nothing you can do to alter your worth.

One time, my college bestie got fed up with the out-loud part of my spin cycles and said to me one morning after I voiced how much I hated myself for drinking the night before, "You do this every time. It's torture. Either stop the morning-after, negative self-talk or stop drinking!" So I stopped the negative self-talk—out loud at least.

My inner dialogue of self-bashing got louder and louder in time. Until finally, the pain of staying the same became greater than the pain of changing.

My search for a solution to quitting alcohol led me to a 3:00 a.m. prayer, which led to an Internet search, which led me to my first support meeting. That evening, I had drunk several glasses of red wine while completing three kids' back-to-school paperwork, which in that season was quite overwhelming to me when added to the other important and menial tasks accompanying being a mom, wife, and good daughter. So, although terrified, at age thirty-seven, I walked into a 12-step meeting attempting to calm my "hangxiety."

I knew no one in recovery. I thought an anonymous 12-step meeting was for drunks living under a bridge chugging from a paper bag. I was raised by teetotaling parents whose parents and extended families also never drank alcohol. Attending a 12-step meeting had never crossed my mind. I had never been called out as having addictive behavior. I just knew deep in my soul that my relationship with alcohol wasn't serving me. I knew, and felt undoubtedly in my gut, it would be the end of me if I continued.

Yet when I asked my doctor about my drinking, he told me there was no problem or threat to my physical health. I asked a therapist about it and was told I had a tendency toward addiction but did not have an addiction, *so just be careful.* I asked my pastor about it and was directed to a Christian version of the 12-step program. I asked the Christian 12-step program leader about it and was told my main problem was being codependent. I asked Scott about it, and he said, "You just need a little coaching. Let's practice going out and drinking only half a martini with dinner."

This was the culture and community I lived in, in 2007. Well-meaning loved ones were giving the best advice they knew how to. Alcoholics Anonymous and rehab were the only well-known solutions to a questionable relationship with alcohol and, as far as I knew, were reserved for serious problem drinkers who had embarrassed themselves and others in public, done jail time, and lost everything—*not* churchgoing, classroom-helper moms like me. It didn't occur to me that my alcohol use was a real problem because, on the surface, I didn't fit the cultural stereotype of the moment. Also, the solution according to both AA and rehab was black and white. You either die from alcohol abuse or admit you have a disease called alcoholism and survive by abstaining completely, attending meetings, and embracing sobriety as a grateful person in recovery. That sounded extreme and not for *someone like me*.

Today there are other options for people curious about cutting alcohol out of their lives. I'll list some in chapter 12 and why it's important to know whether you're wired to thrive with choices such as moderation, abstinence for health reasons, or abstinence for survival. For me, both moderation and abstaining from alcohol merely for wellness or dignity's sake was a green light giving me permission to partake for the "right" occasion or the "right" strength of a craving. The fact is, I am among those who must abstain for survival. I didn't understand this about myself until years later, so I am thankful that in 2007 my options, as far as I knew, were either you're a normie or you're not. I needed the all-or-nothing solution presented to me.

All the trying on my own to figure out how to moderate alcohol exhausted and almost killed me. I wanted fiercely to be a normie. I worked at it—made spreadsheets for my drinks, used baking tools to measure my intake, and created endless rules for my consumption, such as only beer and wine, only after 5:00 p.m., only on weekends, and more. I thought if I could measure my intake, I could control it.

I didn't want to be a drunk. I didn't want to be forced into recovery. I didn't want to get labeled an alcoholic. I didn't want to be a monster. I wanted to be a fun, controlled, dignified social drinker, like media and alcohol marketers portray. I believed then that being a teetotaler would make me the weirdo. The drinking culture was even more persuasive then than it is now, and I was a sucker for it. I believed that if I couldn't partake in drinking the way those around me could, I was weak-willed and something was wrong with me. I believed that since I couldn't sip a martini and then leave it on the bar the way a Bond girl could, I failed. So I gave being a classy drinker my all, never realizing that working tirelessly toward my goal contradicted my image of a failed drunk. I didn't see the driven achiever in all of it. I didn't notice that in every other area of my life discipline and willpower were not issues. I woke up at 5:00 every morning to run before the kids woke, kept a tidy home, was chief administrator of our family finances, and flossed after every meal. Yet I chose to focus on the one thing I couldn't control, then vilified myself for it. I only saw the drunk, so the narrative of my life before finding a sober solution became, *I am an undignified monster.* (I'll cover tools for separating truth from story in chapter 5.)

I wallowed in this narrative from shortly after that first sip of alcohol my freshman year in high school until age thirty-seven when I finally found a solution to the chaos. And for me, I was and am grateful that my choices were all or nothing—continue to be unsuccessful at attempts to moderate my alcohol intake or quit drinking altogether. I did not need more tips on how to drink with elegance or science-backed reasons for not drinking. I needed to know others like me—for whom drinking could kill them. I needed to know there were others like me—well-meaning achievers who've given the drinking culture their all and still cannot normalize alcohol. I needed to know there is nothing wrong or weak about me because of this, and I am worthy even though I am unable to moderate alcohol consumption. I needed to change the monster narrative.

The morning of September 24, 2007, I walked into my first meeting, and it became day one of my sobriety. I didn't look back or question what people told me to do. I stumbled into the group as a last resort. Even though my rock bottom looked different than I thought it was supposed to, I had hit it. Out of options and ideas for how else to get help, I went to the group for what I considered to be serious drunks. I'm thankful God led me there because, to my relief, the room was filled with women I related to—and they had all their teeth. The only requirement for being there was "a desire not to drink!" Immediately, I knew I'd found a solution that worked to a problem that wasn't working. I moved forward, grateful for the lifesaving program and information I discovered. The women I met that morning were the first people to understand the unrest I felt in my soul. They got me and my relationship with alcohol. They articulately explained what I'd been searching to know. These fellow "alcoholic" strangers had walked in my shoes—on the same path the people closest to me throughout my entire life had not traveled. I felt home. Let me note here that I'll come back to the "alcoholic" label in the next chapter. I know it's a loaded one.

You're valuable and worthy exactly where you are at.

On my own, I thought I was letting God help me stop. With the group, I learned *how* to let God help me stop. The first day of my sobriety was the most pivotal day of my search for contentment within my soul up to that point. I learned I wasn't giving something up; I was gaining a beginning to a story in which I'd uncover my authentic self and create the identity I wanted.

On that September day, in a meeting hall dense with the smell of burnt coffee and promise, a woman in the group said the words that sent decades of shame flying off my shoulders: "It is not your fault. You are alcoholic. It is like an allergy." What she said next made my freshly unburdened soul so light I felt like a snow-white apparition hovering above the meeting room's card table and folding chairs. "You never have to have another drink again." For me, a drink meant trying to control. I was tired and out of any more control. This was an unimaginable exhale.

I was ready to hear that I "never *have* to have another drink again." Some people enter recovery and hear, "I never *get* to have another drink again." Neither is right or wrong. You're valuable and worthy exactly where you are at. You could show up to recovery out of exhaustion for trying to quit on your own, like I did. Or you could show up because of a court order or a loved one's nudge out of fear for you. Quitting your thing may still feel like a chore instead of a relief, and that is what it is. Either way you are brave for reading this book and showing up instead of checking out.

For me, being told I was alcoholic and that it was like an allergy was freeing. I was off the hook. If I had this thing that had a name, I could find a solution to it. I immediately moved out of the problem and into the solution. This truth that I was an alcoholic did not make me want to grow even more active in my addiction. Because the comradery and connection were so positive, I became a reassured alcoholic, active in recovery. It was a badge of inclusion connecting me with the first people I'd ever met on my same frequency.

I was finally free from the distraction of drinking, moderating, or not drinking alcohol. I was exhausted from fighting to control something that clearly controlled me.

Guilt Assessment

Here is an exercise to help you examine the rules you create for achieving your standards and the guilt or shame that may follow when you don't reach them.

- First, determine if your guilt is natural or harmful by stating the standard you believe you're missing. My standard was: I want to be and feel like a worthy person.
- Is this standard realistic and attainable? (Mine was.) What has to happen for you to accomplish that standard? What do you or others have to do, if anything? These are the rules you've set for yourself. These are the things that must happen for your standards to be met.
- My rule was: To be and feel worthy, I need to quit drinking. Since I didn't know how to quit drinking, I didn't feel worthy. Feeling worthy is a fine standard. The problem was in the rule I set for feeling worthy. In this case, the guilt I felt for not being able to quit was harmful, because feeling worthy depended on something that was outside of my ability to do on my own at that time; thus, I made feeling worthy impossible.

- Write each of your own standards and rules for hitting them as bullet points. Take each rule and ask yourself, *Is this rule within my control to accomplish or does it depend on someone or something outside of my control to make it happen?*
- For me, the truth was, I was worthy before I learned how to quit drinking. Knowing this made it easier to partner with a supportive community that showed me a solution.
- If reaching your set standard depends on circumstances or people outside of your control, or if it depends on an unrealistic or unattainable effort on your part, then you are setting a nearly impossible standard. For example, if your standard is to feel happy, and your rule for feeling happy is that others include you and like you, then you have made happiness unlikely to achieve because you cannot control other people's opinions of you or your choices.

There is nothing you can do or think to negate your worth, and shame holds no power, right, or authority in your life.

- If your rule for feeling happy is that you start your day with meditation and exercise, then you have set an attainable standard because it is within your ability to achieve. If you experience guilt for not exercising one day, you can acknowledge it, show yourself grace, then use that guilt to fuel you to do even better going forward (natural guilt). If you feel guilt for not getting invited to a social event, you are stuck because being included is outside of your control (harmful guilt).

- Once you have set attainable standards, notice if you experience a guilty feeling. Next, stop and celebrate that you're aware of your feelings; then go through the previous list to see if you made an unreasonable rule for yourself. If so, ditch the guilt. It's human to feel guilt even when there are no grounds for it. However, it will not serve you to hang on to that type of guilt.
- If, however, the guilt assessment shows a true indication that you need to change and redirect your actions, do so and move on.
- Perhaps not meeting standards has moved beyond guilt to believing either consciously or subconsciously that you are a bad person. When beating yourself up shifts from holding yourself accountable to impossible standards into believing you are trash for not reaching them, shame is alive.

Shame is a liar. Regardless of how high or low you set your standards and whether or not you reach them, you are worthy and loved and whole. You are a priceless treasure whether you are addicted or sober, guilty or innocent, sick or healthy, stalled or growing, seeking or knowing. There is nothing you can do or think to negate your worth, and shame holds no power, right, or authority in your life.

Chapter 2

It's Not Your Fault

*Even in recent years, I have seen too many people
I loved struggle with addiction and die tragically
from this epidemic. It is time for us to say goodbye
to shame about addiction. We have to stop blaming
and judging ourselves and the people around
us.... That starts with sharing our stories.*[2]
—Lisa Marie Presley

THE MESSAGE THAT ADDICTIONS ARE A PHYSIO-logical issue and not a moral issue, delivered by the sober angel of a woman at my first meeting, was gold for me. This truth replaced my shame with certainty and created a foundation of empowering beliefs that followed.

Maybe you picked up this book because you know logically you are worthy and loved, yet there is some behavior that leaves you feeling otherwise. We will explore your beliefs together, and I'll coach you through creating powerful narratives that serve you and your goals.

Perhaps the thing you know deep down you'd be better without isn't alcohol like mine was. We will name your "thing" in chapter 4 and work through steps to breaking your stronghold. I'll use my own examples with alcohol to share how you can get unstuck and move forward for yourself.

Look, addiction is hard for those of us who got caught in its trap. But it doesn't have to be. Nobody becomes addicted until they engage in a thing for the first time. If you, like me, did get caught in an addictive snare, know that it is not your fault. It is the fault of the addictive thing. The thing, not you, has the flaw. Granted, you are responsible for stopping the cycle, but not because it's your fault it started; rather, between you and the habit, you are the smarter one. You, along with your Creator and a supportive community, are capable of breaking free from whatever wants to keep you trapped. You'll do this with grit plus heaps of grace for yourself. I'll help you.

One magical thing about sharing our stories is, while we each have a different one, we hear parts of our own stories in the stories of others, and those similarities remind us we are not alone. The more we share, the greater our reach to those on our frequency and the more souls we get to touch and be touched by. Part of my recovery story that I'll share in part 2 is that after thirteen-plus years of living free from the distraction of alcohol, I managed to forget what it was like to be tripped up—like the person who takes a multivitamin to feel better, then feels better and so decides they no longer need the vitamin. I invited alcohol back into my life and soon remembered that being tripped up sucks. I fiercely missed my sobriety, yet getting it back was not as simple as protecting it when I had it. Staying sober is way more fun than getting sober. Though getting sober a second time was hard, it was not as hard as not doing it would have been. I *chose* my hard, and I'll help you choose yours.

We hear parts of our own stories in the stories of others, and those similarities remind us we are not alone.

Today I understand that the gifts recovery gave me are my fuel to stay sober, not a sign I have outgrown the need for it. While I wouldn't recommend you go on the same field trip as me, I believe my drinking-curious experiment was not without purpose. I hope my experience, and lessons learned, will inspire and equip you to find understanding within a like-minded community and move into forward action.

I'm not here to determine right from wrong for you. I want to share my tools with you. When establishing the patterns that move you toward, and keep you living the life you want, there is no right versus wrong, only helpful versus unhelpful. I don't have answers for you; I have questions for you. Coaches are trained to question, not to tell. I'll ask questions throughout this book to help you tap in to your cleverness. I'll share my story and help you get curious about yours.

When it comes to absorbing self-help, I'm a fan of "if it moves you toward what you want, keep it. If it doesn't, dump it." Use what works for you and allow others to use what works for them. Take in as much information as you desire, then keep what works. And if what works for you changes over time, evolve with those changes. Your past is not wrong. It launched you to the place you are now and your seasons yet to come.

The tricky thing about writing self-help is I'm keenly aware of how much I don't know yet. The awareness that what I know today will change tomorrow is enough to pause my writing if I let it. I want to share what's working *now*. Let's stay curious and grow together.

To determine which patterns to pick up and which to toss, ask yourself, *Is this behavior or thought moving me toward the life I want or not?* If not, ditch it. Now, I realize that's easier said than done. That's OK. We are going to move together through getting crystal clear on what you want, then creating a strategy to reach what you want. I'll provide tools to hang up your hang-ups with grit plus grace. Reading this book as you shift from a pattern that no longer serves you to one that does is an invigorating way to forge a fresh focus.

Framework for Sharing

A guideline for sharing one's story in a 12-step meeting is to share one's experience, strength, and hope by being honest about three things: What it was like, what happened, and what it is like now. In recovery this means what it was like when the speaker was active in their addiction, what happened to alert them there was a different way, and what it's like now that they are free.

This book uses a similar format to tell my story. What it was like for me to embrace sobriety, what happened to make me question the necessity of my alcohol-free life-style, and what it's like now that I've learned to appreciate recovery in a new and even brighter light. Most importantly, I share how my personal experience, coupled with my coach training, will help you gain physical and emotional sobriety from whatever is hindering you from living the life you want and will help you embrace the grace you deserve.

For years, I did not want to ingest any new information about sobriety. I did not want to expose my mind to new or different ways of thinking about drinking or not drinking—because my 12-step program was working for me. It stopped working when I became a coach and got curious enough to question my *why* for being sober (more on this in chapter 7). It was time for me to evolve with the new information I had learned. I needed to rewrite my *why*.

If you are already enjoying a program that works for you, keep going. Keep doing what is already working. If, however, you are in a curious space and questioning your relationship with a ritual, either for the first time or again after stringing together years of continuous abstinence, this book will help guide your curiosity.

Whatever you decide works for you, be certain it involves community. Find a community of people who share your goals (I'll help you with this in chapter 12). The common denominator throughout my seventeen-year-long recovery journey thus far has been community. I believe that the role alcohol plays in society today makes it difficult to abstain from it on one's own. I also believe this will change in the future. Young adults today are already choosing not to drink alcohol, some before even trying it. A 2023 article in *Billboard* magazine quotes David Slutes, the entertainment director for the 325-capacity Club Congress in Tucson, Arizona, as saying, "We weren't sure why the numbers were like this. Then we did a deeper dive, and at every event aimed at a Gen Z crowd, we saw numbers that were very different. Gen Z'ers are just simply not drinking the same amount [as their predecessors]."[3]

There are several reasons not to imbibe poison, and society is beginning to recognize those reasons. If, however, you grew up in an indulgent culture, as I did, a support community will make shifting the patterns your brain has created around a ritual easier and more fun. Turning from what's toxic toward what's life-giving is entirely possible, and a supportive community invigorates movement toward the life you want.

A Word about Words

Now, a few words about words—especially the *A* word. Once we label ourselves, we often give ourselves an excuse to fall deeper into our addiction or fly above it. Labels can serve us or hurt us. The "alcoholic" label, for example, can look like: *Oh well, I am an alcoholic, just like my parents were. I'm doomed to continue in this addictive trap.* Or, *I'm an alcoholic just like millions of others and thank God I'm not alone. I'm part of a community of alcoholics who have identified a problem to move into its solution together.* Change the label, change the narrative. If you have been caught in an addictive trap, give yourself loads of grace and seek help from others who've been where you are.

As humans we love labels. I've been surprised that some readers' favorite part of my first book, *Living All In: How to Show Up for the Life You Want,* was when I shared about being a highly sensitive person (HSP). People love being able to identify with something. However, we must be careful that what we identify as leads where we want to go, not where we want to move away from. Identifying with a label is different from making a label your identity.

> **Identifying with a label is different from making a label your identity.**

Personally, I am not stunted by the alcoholic label. I never thought about the word in relation to myself before that first meeting, so it landed on me in an energetic and healing way. I understand this is not the case for every person. For me, it explained a part of myself I'd been struggling to understand for years. It was a relief to know my hang-up had a name. It moved my monster out of the dark and served me to know I am not alone. Being told in a meeting I am alcoholic was as easy as being told I am allergic to a certain food. It defined my severe reaction to a thing, took the shame off it, and provided a prescription for survival.

The "alcoholics" I surround myself with are thriving in long-term sobriety. In 12-step meetings, I identify as an alcoholic proudly because we alcoholics share a common language. When I say, "I'm Chris, an alcoholic," others know it is a positive term that unites a room full of sober superstars doing life together.

Outside of 12-step meetings, I rarely use the alcoholic label because too many people associate it with being in an active addiction. It can conjure up a lushy boozehound image for some, and I don't want to cause confusion or cause others to stumble. Also, I do not need to label myself in order not to drink. I've grown out of believing I'm the weirdo for not drinking and now believe it's ridiculous to have to explain not ingesting a drug. I do not need to explain why I say no to cocaine or meth or tobacco, so why should I explain not drinking poison to anyone?

Once, I experimented in front of a mirror by saying this: "Hi, I'm Chris and I choose sobriety." While true—I choose sobriety because it's more fun, more exciting, and more life-giving for me than a life that includes alcohol—the label is not a safety seal. What happens if I decide not to choose sobriety one day? What happens if I decide to follow a craving and choose a drink under the illusion that the choice is simple? For me and others like me, one drink can be fatal. Since the choice is life or death—sobriety versus a leap of faith in my ability to control alcohol, a thing that has the power to control me—knowing I'm "alcoholic" frees me from having to willpower my way into drinking or not drinking. Honoring the way I am lets me off the hook from having to choose.

Just because my first association with the word *alcoholic* was healing and positive doesn't mean yours was or is. It also doesn't mean that the *A* word will not change for me over time. It's important to label or not label yourself in line with what works best for you to thrive. Language is ever-evolving. Ask yourself what words move you forward, keep you stuck in a loop, or reroute you backward. When you're trying on words for yourself, notice how they make you feel, then keep what serves you and dump what doesn't.

For example, in early recovery I questioned the term *normie*. As a sober person I wanted to normalize the alcohol-free lifestyle, but the term seemed to do the opposite. However, *normal* means typical, standard, usual, or expected. It is the mainstream. I live in a world where alcohol use is mainstream, so someone who can partake in that lifestyle without consequences is standard— normal. I, on the other hand, have an abnormal response to alcohol and there are consequences when I drink it. So the term *normie* makes sense to me and helps me make sense of the differences between my response to alcohol and the average person's response to alcohol. Plus, being different is exciting to me. What matters is what makes sense to you. Think about how words land on you. Does a term help you make sense of your relationship to a habit, or does it confuse you?

Different labels, sober communities, and recovery options exist because unique people exist. There is not one church for all people, one way to grieve for all people, or one therapist, coach, counselor, or mentor for all people. There is not one recovery language for all people. If there were, too many folks would be left without options for help. Debate over words such as *alcoholic*, *disease*, *normie*, *sobriety*, and *recovery* being right or wrong is not helpful. Writers volunteer to serve their audience by sharing (most often uncomfortably) their experiences, knowing that content will not serve every person. I'm equipped to share my experience, coaching tools, and what works for me. I was addicted to alcohol, and I am not anymore. There are no guarantees that I won't become addicted again, so I honor my recovery through writing, being of service to others, and staying close to my sober community. I don't mind what people label that. I care about my sobriety and yours. The tools in this book are meant to ignite your resourcefulness and creativity to get clear on what works and does not work for *you*, not ignite a debate over language.

Focus on what works, not what hasn't worked in the past.

Please focus on the similarities of our stories instead of the differences. If you want to gain freedom, focus on what works, not what hasn't worked in the past, and you'll be set to soar.

Chapter 3

Party People

You didn't want to make things perfect.
You just hated things the way they are.
—Rocket Raccoon, *Guardians of the Galaxy Vol. 3*

WHEN I FOUND FRIENDS I COULD RELATE TO IN support groups, it felt like I had found lost family members. Meeting others who shared several of my character traits felt like, *Oh, there you are. I've been looking for you*. It was as though others joined my party—then moved it from my head to the dance floor. And when the party got more exhausting than fun, the people on my wavelength made dancing through the dips and leaps doable. Life is just easier when you realize you're in sync with others.

What do I mean by "in sync"? Some of us in recovery share more than just our addiction. Here are a few character traits that I've noticed are often common to people in recovery. If any of these sound familiar to you, it's time to get out of your head and hit the dance floor. You are not alone.

Perfectionism and High Achievement

Although often found in combination, there is a difference between a high achiever and a perfectionist. A high achiever can be flexible and resilient, whereas a perfectionist is often rigid and self-critical. Driven achievers are pulled toward their goals because they want to reach them and are usually pleased with their forward progress. Perfectionists tend to be pushed by a fear of anything less than a perfectly met goal. When that is the case, perfectionism is destructive since perfection is unattainable— at least this side of eternity. Destructive perfectionism includes all-or-nothing thinking, being highly critical of self and others, feeling pushed by fear, setting unrealistic standards, procrastination, fear of failure, and feeling depressed when goals aren't met.

I am a driven achiever who used to get in tight spots from perfectionistic thinking. If you are a perfectionist, don't fret. It is a powerful trait if you use your tendencies in helpful ways. Perfectionism can be both constructive and destructive.

In her book *The Perfectionist's Guide to Losing Control*, psychotherapist Katherine Morgan Schafler describes perfectionists as "people who consistently notice the difference between an ideal and a reality, and who strive to maintain a high degree of personal accountability. This results in the perfectionist experiencing, more often than not, a compulsion to bridge the gulf between reality and an ideal themselves."[4] She goes on to empower the perfectionist by explaining, "With the capacity to be expressed in both constructive and destructive ways, perfectionism is a natural human impulse that we animate through our thoughts, behaviors, feelings, and interpersonal relationships. Persisting across time and cultures, the universal desire to actualize the ideals we imagine is as healthy as the impulse to love, to solve problems, to make art, to kiss, to tell stories, and so on."[5]

Like many natural instincts, perfectionism gets us in tight spots when we let it. Destructive perfectionism causes problems when our expectations of how someone or something should be are not met. Unmet expectations often lead to anger, frustration, and resentment.

As a high achiever who grew up a destructive perfectionist, I am quick to see correlations between perfectionism and getting caught in an addictive trap. As rigid, all-or-nothing thinkers, we get ourselves stuck by setting standards impossibly difficult to achieve and tragically easy not to achieve. We make feeling good impossibly hard and feeling bad tragically easy. When we can't solve this lose-lose conundrum, we numb, appease, or soothe ourselves with a temporary solution. Over time that solution becomes a ritual, then an addiction.

Let's flip this. What *realistic and attainable* thing can you do right now that will bring satisfaction, joy, and contentment? Do it, then celebrate yourself. Now do the next thing.

For years, I set standards that were impossibly hard to reach. I made it tragically easy to feel cruddy about myself. When I was young this happened with food. I would say, "I am not going to eat ___" or "I am only going to eat ___ today." I was in high school during the eighties, when the world was not as informed about health as it is now. Being healthy meant being skinny, and the way to achieve skinny was to cut calories to below a healthy recommendation.

Limiting my daily calorie intake was one of the standards I held myself to as a young woman. It was not wrong. It was the best I knew to do with what I knew about nutrition at the time. I was skinny, happy with my weight and appearance, and had the brainpower of a crazed lunatic.

The problem with rigid thinking is, it sucks when you're able to achieve it and sucks even more when you don't. It's a lose-lose. If I am craving a hearty meal and depriving myself, I lose. If I am craving a hearty meal and engaging, going against the low-calorie standard I set for myself, I also lose, because now I'm in a shame spiral. I'm beating myself up for not holding to the rule I set for myself. Judgment, blame, and rules stink. They keep you stuck.

The way this looked later in life with alcohol went like this: *I said I wasn't going to drink last night. I did. I broke my ___ day sobriety streak. Now I'm back at day one. This sucks. Since I'm already a hopeless loser with no willpower, I'll go ahead and drink again. I can start my day one another time.* The worst part is, once I think I'm a hopeless loser, I'll act like one. If I already blew it, I may as well go out with a bang and start over tomorrow—or the day, week, or month after that. I may as well go on a bender.

Trade beating yourself up with curiosity. Dig deep and ask yourself questions: *What do I want? How do I want to feel? What food, behaviors, or substances get me to that feeling?*

When you experience an unhelpful feeling, stop and ask yourself, *What story am I telling myself right now?*

What else? You don't lift yourself up by beating yourself up. The exercise in chapter 4 will help you get even more curious about these questions and your answers.

Asking questions is key to unlocking what you want and discovering what drives you toward or prevents you from getting where you want to go. I'll be asking questions throughout this book to help you tap into your own resourcefulness and stay curious about what works to move toward your desired outcomes. Productive curiosity will move you forward.

One of my favorite questions to ask clients when I hear they are stuck in a limiting belief is, "Is that true?" When you experience an unhelpful feeling, stop and ask yourself, *What story am I telling myself right now?* If the story you're telling yourself isn't serving you, question it. Ask yourself, *Is that true?* Rewrite a narrative to move you forward. We will dive deeper into the stories we tell ourselves that narrate our self-worth, and how to rewrite them, in chapter 5.

Asking questions helps people unlock their positive curiosity and find their own answers. Asking ourselves questions does the same. Discovering our own answers fosters a self-awareness that sticks far more than being told what to do will. Choose what sticks instead of being stuck.

High Sensitivity

As a young person, my inability not to "be so sensitive" became a second problem on top of being sensitive, which I used to think was wrong. I looked for ways to numb the feeling of inadequacy the "oversensitive" label gave me—as if I were less than because I felt things deeply. I tried various numbing potions: food, excessive exercise, and alcohol. These potions were solutions—until they weren't.

In 1991 when I graduated from college, clinical psychologist Elaine Aron coined the term *highly sensitive person* (HSP). Once I realized others like me were out there, I felt strengthened. (Several resources are now available on the subject should you want to learn more.)

A highly sensitive person has a finely wired central nervous system and an increased awareness of physical, emotional, and social stimuli. Some HSP traits include:
- being deeply moved by beauty
- avoiding violent movies or television shows because they feel too intense and unsettling

- needing downtime
- having a rich and complex inner life with deep thoughts and strong feelings
- having a tough time receiving negative feedback
- freezing under pressure
- experiencing analysis paralysis
- exhibiting high creativity
- being detail-oriented
- having a high propensity for empathy (often having a deep empathetic and even physical response to what others think and feel)
- possessing the gift of intuition
- being overwhelmed by sensory stimuli, such as noisy crowds, bright lights, or uncomfortable clothing (I call this one the "Princess and the Pea Phenomenon")

Check, check, and check! For me, knowing the HSP label exists freed my soul, much like learning I was alcoholic did. I realized I wasn't inadequate, broken, or weird. I didn't need a remedy for my sensitivity. The "sensitive" label fit, and learning how to embrace it in healthy ways was a good thing.

I'm grateful for the strengths being a highly sensitive person gives me. I've learned how to manage this label well and celebrate the way I am wired.

Managing my HSP well includes healthy acknowledgment of the positives of this label and not using it as an excuse for unproductive behavior. Although acknowledging my tendency might mean I say no to some things, if I were to regularly say to others, "I'm a highly sensitive person, so I cannot partake in this or that activity," I would become a hindrance to them and miss out on my growth. I wouldn't push myself to live outside the "Princess and the Pea" description. I would be using the HSP label as an excuse to stay inside my comfort zone.

> **Use how you are made as fuel instead of being used by your unique design. In other words, you get to control the narrative of your wiring.**

Use how you are made as fuel instead of being used by your unique design. In other words, you get to control the narrative of your wiring. You can find the beauty and strengths in your unique makeup, or you can allow it to limit you. You get to choose how loud and proud you live!

Balance, Rhythm, and Teeter-Totters

In an attempt for the ideal, rigid thinkers often disregard the real. The craving is real. The desire is real. Our faults and flubs are real. The beauty of human nature lies in the real, not the ideal. Striving for balance only adds another layer of something to strive for. We risk making balance our new ideal. If this is the case, what happens when we don't strike a balance? We've set yet another standard that, if not reached, will cast us into a pit of shame, guilt, and told-you-sos.

Instead of balance, aim to achieve a rhythm. This is a far kinder way to get where you want to go. Balance risks one tiny factor throwing you off. Think of a teeter-totter. There's only up or down. To achieve an in-between, level balance, circumstances on either side must be perfect. And you're in control of only one side. Even if you achieve perfect control of your teeter, you have zero control of the totter. Attempting balance puts tremendous pressure on you and unrealistic pressure on others and circumstances outside of your control.

Rhythm is a cadence you can dance to. It allows for dips and twirls and the unexpected. When you dance to the rhythm of your life, accepting all the twists and turns, you'll position yourself to get where you want to go. You'll bridge the gap from where you are to what you want, and you'll do this with heaps of grace for yourself, others, and your circumstances along the way.

How do we get off the teeter-totter and on the dance floor? Start with trading expectations for appreciation. Anger is most often a result of an unmet expectation. When we expect ourselves, others, or a circumstance to be one way and it plays out a different way, we become angry. If anger isn't an emotion you want, practice appreciating how things are going instead of focusing on how you expect them to go. Believe that life happens *for* you instead of *to* you. Trust that when you show up for your life as it is, instead of how you think it should be, you'll have everything you need in each moment to dance through it.

Instead of balance, aim to achieve a rhythm. This is a far kinder way to get where you want to go.

Having strength to move through difficult events does not mean that moving through them won't suck.

And if we show up instead of checking out, we will move forward. Feeling our feelings is not for wimps, and you are not a wimp.

If you're thinking, *Easy for you to say, Chris*, then try it anyway. You'll be surprised at the strength you'll muster when you trust that you will have what you need to keep going. Trust doesn't mean it worked out as you expect it to. It means believing the way it worked out, though painful, will not crush you.

This concept becomes easier if you have faith in a higher power and trust that divine power is rooted in love. Love works in the favor of those who trust its power. Unfair, hard, or difficult circumstances don't become less sucky when we trust our higher power. But trusting will give us what we need to maneuver through seemingly unbearable situations instead of checking out of them.

Approval Junkiness

When you perform to receive or avoid a reaction from others, you will strive to strike a balance between what is enough and not enough. Since that perfect balance does not exist, you risk sneaking or skirting the truth (lying to yourself and others) to manipulate another person's reaction. You disrespect yourself to gain a false dignity from an outside source.

In addition to the standards we already set for ourselves, society has set standards for us. Are we too much or not enough? As a young woman I was confused. Was I too thin or not thin enough? Were my outfits too skimpy or too frumpy? Was I too loud or not fun enough? Was I too loose-lipped or not vulnerable enough? Too public or too private? Did I talk too much or not enough? Did I drink too much or not enough? The constant searching for balance was exhausting.

I think this is where we get the popular phrase "you are enough." Women, especially, are spent by the quest to figure out the formula for how to be elegant and dignified without being uptight. Being told we are "enough" solves the equation and shuts down the figuring. The truth is, though, you don't need to be enough of anything. It is your human right to just be. You are.

Comparison

Now that you are off the hook to be enough, and free just to be, you will never compare yourself to others again—right? I'm laughing while writing because I wish it were easy to stop comparing myself to others and my ideal self.

Comparison springs organically in me whether I'm conscious of it or not. Comparison creeps up and, if I'm not vigilant, will take me down. It ran rampant in me as a young woman. I even compared myself to past romanticized versions of me. This looked like longing to be at the same weight or fitness level as I was in high school or believing I should look the same in my mom outfits as I did in my college ones or have the same energy at fifty as I did at twenty.

If you are wired for high growth, you'll naturally measure yourself against perceived ideals. Though it's not wrong, it may not be helpful if the ideal is not realistic or attainable. The trick is to change the perception and ideal without stunting your growth mindset.

To do this, first recognize when you're comparing. If you feel unsettled, discontent, frustrated with yourself, or find yourself spending more energy on what another is doing than on your own pursuits, stop and celebrate your awareness. Next, get curious. What or who were you focused on? Now that you've brought the object of your comparison to your conscious mind, set it aside and direct the focus to the next best thing for *you* to do.

One way to do this is to ask your higher power what is the next best thing. Pray for your desires for yourself to line up with your higher power's desires for you. Perform for an "audience of one" rather than an audience of strangers and unrealistic expectations. Pastor Craig Groeschel shared this gem on Instagram: "Comparison will either make you feel superior or inferior. Neither honors God."[6]

Imposter Syndrome

Early in my coach training, I dwelled studiously on my plan for getting the client their outcome until I'd fumble with imposter syndrome. I listened more intently to the ramblings in my head than to what the client was saying. This stemmed from a deep want to be a good coach. I wanted to be as skilled as my teachers. That desire to be as good as those who'd gone before me was not wrong. It's a character trait of being driven for growth. It was not serving me, however, because it was selfish. I was more focused on comparing myself to other coaches and the coach I wished to be than I was on my client. The moment I realized this I became an efficient coach that gets her clients the results they want. I turned my light bulb moment into an affirmation that goes like this:

I focus on the client's outcome, not my ability to get their outcome.

This works with any type of performance. Whether you are speaking, singing, playing sports, or socializing, focus on the person you are meant to serve, not on your ability to serve them.

Visualizing your peak performance and the result you want is an effective tool, to be certain. I wrote about this in *Living All In*. That is different, however, than dwelling on your ability to get a result by comparing yourself to others or longing for an unrealistic version of you. Either way, focus on the result you want. If the result you want is a fantastic outcome for a person you are serving, then your focus must be on that person.

Focusing on how you'll perform keeps you comparing yourself to others and your own ideals. Focusing on who you're performing for gives you a servant's heart. When you're in your head, you're dead. When you live to give, you're living all in.

Apologizing

On one of my morning runs, a leashed dog being walked lunged toward me. Dodging the lunge, I tripped from sidewalk to street calling out, "I'm so sorry!" The dog and its owner continued past me with no response. Why did I instinctively and immediately apologize for another's action? Not only did I place the fault on myself in that moment, I caught myself thinking about it later during the run. I thought, *I hope that person knows I'm sorry.* What in the world!? Did the walker's silence leave me longing for closure and forgiveness?

Why did I crave a pointless pardon? Why was I energetically and emotionally tangled by a stranger? Why did I care?

Had my logical husband (or perhaps some of you reading this) been there, he would have asked why I apologized and may have even exchanged unpleasantries with the dog walker who paid no mind to my falter.

There are judicious assumptions as to why I apologized for the derailing lurch—from the personality type I was born with to patterns developed in childhood such as apologizing for myself because that is what I could control when threatened by what I could not control, such as the actions of others (or an inquisitive dog).

Saying "I'm sorry" often and unthinkingly, however, dilutes the sincerity of deserving apologies.

I am less concerned with why I offered the unmerited plea than I am delighted that I noticed it and have the tools to reframe the incident. What I am certain of is that catching myself in a backassward apology allows me to stop and celebrate my awareness and then move on. By the end of my run, I was over it. Curious enough to write about it, but over it.

Is this story familiar to you? I've met several practiced apologizers in recovery. Those of us who have created soothing rituals to cope with or avoid unwanted feelings or circumstances are experts at controlling what we can when we feel out of control with what is not our right to manage. In the same way, being quick to apologize for our part, warranted or not, comes naturally because it is within our control.

One way to replace unwarranted knee-jerk apologies with something different is to replace "I'm sorry" with "Thank you."

Of course, some forgiveness must be asked for, and having the humility to authentically say "I'm sorry" is vital. Saying "I'm sorry" often and unthinkingly, however, dilutes the sincerity of deserving apologies. So how do we spot the unnecessary apologies?

Author and coach Mel Robbins wrote four reasons not to say "I'm sorry":

1. Saying "I'm sorry" is annoying. "I'm sorry I talk too much." "I'm sorry my house is a mess." Notice how many times you say "I'm sorry" today.

2. Saying "I'm sorry" makes you the center of attention. "I'm sorry I'm so high maintenance." "I'm sorry I missed your birthday." Notice how everyone turns to you as soon as you start apologizing.

3. Saying "I'm sorry" is your way of seeking reassurance. "I'm sorry I can't make it." "I'm sorry I'm late." When you apologize, you're hoping someone says, "It's OK."

4. Saying "I'm sorry" gives your power away. "I'm sorry but I have a question." "I'm sorry, can you explain that again?" When you apologize for your existence, you belittle your needs.[7]

Robbins suggests saying "thank you" instead of "I'm sorry" to take your power back and show others that you appreciate their support. She writes, "Instead of 'I'm sorry I'm late,' say, 'Thank you for your patience.'"

People deserve to hear thank you instead of I'm sorry. Others deserve to be acknowledged for their support of you rather than asked for their attention to you. And you have the wisdom to know the difference between what you cannot change and what you can.

Memorize the first part of the serenity prayer by Reinhold Niebuhr, which is common in recovery groups, as a helping hand to elevate you to the sidewalk should you involuntarily trip into the street:

> *God, grant me the serenity*
> *to accept the things I cannot change,*
> *the courage to change the things I can,*
> *and the wisdom to know the difference.*[8]

We cannot change all our circumstances. We can change the stories we attach to them.

People Pleasing

People pleasing isn't about pleasing other people. It's about pleasing ourselves by controlling how others view us. People pleasing seeks feeling good and skirting shame through working not to disappoint others. Once we see that people pleasing is about controlling our own feelings instead of serving others, we can shut down the pattern. Accept that you will not please everyone. If your happiness depends on others liking or agreeing with you, you've set yet another impossible standard to meet.

Avoiding Conflict

When we feel disempowered around prickly personalities, we've meshed the line between their behavior and our feelings. Without helpful tools to soothe our feelings of resentment, frustration, or disempowerment, we may avoid conflict by reaching for alcohol or other harmful soothers to remedy the intensity of our feelings in the presence of thorny folks.

I get a lot of questions from clients about how to deal with difficult personalities, and my favorite answer is, pay attention to the questions and thoughts floating through your conscious and subconscious mind so you can flip what doesn't serve you to something that does. Instead of asking lousy questions such as, *Why is this person doing this to me?*, *Why do they treat me that way?*, or *Why can't they act different?* ask questions that put the narrative back in your jurisdiction, such as, *What do I have control over right now?*, *How do I want to feel right now?*, or *What is within my power to act on right now?* When our minds ask disempowering questions, our brilliant brains will answer the question, and a lousy question will get a lousy answer. For example, if your brain asks, *Why are they doing this to me?* your brain will answer with something like, *Because they have always and will always make me feel this way.* This answer will disarm you and keep you feeling bad because it places the control over your feelings in another person's armory. The truth is, no one is doing anything *to you.* No one has the power to *make* you feel something you don't want to feel unless you grant them that power. They are simply being themselves, and you get to be yourself.

Look, the way to avoid feeling bad in a difficult person's presence is to stand in your power. Do not give your power away to other people to decide how you feel, especially if that person wants to bully you. Bullies have mastered the art of pressing our buttons, and while those buttons may have gotten pressed in the past, they do not need to in the future.

Know that people have a right to say the words they choose to use, and you have a right to decide how those words land on you.

How do you get the "do not press" barrier secured over your button? Know that people have a right to say the words they choose to use, and you have a right to decide how those words land on you. When you feel a way you don't want to feel, use that feeling as an action signal to pause and celebrate your awareness, then ask yourself what thought just went through your mind. Next, reframe it to something that empowers you.

Be in control of the things you have control over (yourself). We do not have control over other people. Let them spin out. Let them do their thing, and you do yours. Setting boundaries is not about what the other person does or does not do; it's about the boundaries you set and what you decide you will accept and not accept. We are not in control of other people. We cannot hold others accountable for stomping on our boundaries. We must be accountable to ourselves instead. It is our responsibility to remove ourselves, ask better questions, or not participate in the insanity and chaos that somebody else is stirring up. Think of it like a hot tub or jacuzzi—there's the insanity that is in the jacuzzi and it's swirling around with bubbles and chaos. You don't have to get in the jacuzzi. You can sit on the side. You don't even have to dip your little toe in! You get to stay on the side within the boundaries you set for yourself.

Stand in your power or sit on the side of the jacuzzi and stop giving your power away to other people to control how you feel. You are the only one in charge of your feelings. You and I get to choose our own thoughts, feelings, beliefs, and actions.

I understand that healthy disengagement can be hard and may cause feelings of guilt. This is natural and does not mean you've made a wrong decision.

> **I understand that healthy disengagement can be hard and may cause feelings of guilt. This is natural and does not mean you've made a wrong decision.**

Note: For matters where disengaging is physically impossible and your safety is a concern, seek help. This paragraph addresses difficult personalities, not abusive crimes, in which case the phone number for the US National Domestic Violence Hotline is 800-799-7233.

Self-Soothing

Self-soothing isn't wrong. It's an act of meeting a basic human need unconsciously or consciously. However, over time the thing we use to meet the need turns to ritualistic comfort seeking, and ritualistic comfort seeking may become a harmful addiction. We all have something we do to meet human needs such as love, connection, comfort, nourishment, belonging, physical touch, certainty, and variety. Some of our harmful addictions started as harmless attempts to meet basic needs. The key is to stay curious and aware of what serves you and what doesn't without villainizing yourself for falling into a snare.

Self-injury, such as cutting, picking, scratching, burning, or biting, is one form of soothing because it brings a brief release of physical and emotional tension. Though it brings a fleeting calm, it is usually followed by guilt and shame. The original tension the self-injury meant to relieve returns, and the cycle continues.

As a kid I picked at my skin, bit the inside of my mouth, and scratched at any bug bite or skin abnormality until it formed a mark. At the time I didn't know I was meeting my need for certainty by substituting a physical feeling I controlled and could be certain of for all kinds of fears and uncertainty. Instead, I believed I was trashy, weak, undisciplined, and less than because picking at my skin left noticeable scars on me.

A vivid memory of mine is one where I was fixating on a fellow camper's legs during worship time at the high school summer camp I attended yearly in the Santa Cruz mountains. Her skin was flawless. Not a scar in sight. I created a narrative about how proud this girl's mother most likely was of her. To me this teenager was elegant, dignified, and represented my personal goal—all because I could tell by her skin that she was not a picker.

I still pick at my skin when I am not on guard. Scott knows instantly if I am concerned about something outside of my control—like something one of the kids is going through—because I start picking. I understand why I picked as a kid and that I don't need to pick anymore. I no longer attach shame or negative self-beliefs to my temptation to pick. I know better than to pick. I don't want to pick. And yet that pattern pops up ritualistically when it's triggered by certain concerns. The difference now is that I recognize it, thank it for showing up like a well-trained comfort dog, and let it know its services are not needed today because I will be turning to healthier coping comforts. Over time the healthier soothers become the new ritual. The old soothers are still present; they just don't hold the same power over me.

However, over time the thing we use to meet the need turns to ritualistic comfort seeking, and ritualistic comfort seeking may become a harmful addiction.

There's nothing wrong with you for having survival and coping instincts that kick in. You're human. And there is a better way for you and me to recognize our triggers and soothe ourselves.

Not all soothers are harmful. Some helpful soothers include meditation, exercise, prayer, talking to a friend, laughing, being in nature, being with animals, and listening to music. In the next chapter you'll get to define in order to shine light on your soothers. Whatever thing you do to meet your human needs is not ugly or shameful. It just isn't serving you anymore, so we will get it out of the dark together.

Chapter 4

Define, Then Shine

*One of our greatest freedoms is
how we react to things.*
—Charlie Mackesy,
*The Boy, the Mole, the Fox
and the Horse*

LIKE THE ENGLISH WORD *LOVE*, THE WORD *SOBER* can mean many things. It can be defined as "not intoxicated," or eating and drinking sparingly, or a "sedate, gravely or earnestly thoughtful character or demeanor." It can mean "unhurried, calm," marked by "temperance, moderation of seriousness." Or it can be "subdued in tone or color," "showing no excessive or extreme qualities of fancy, emotion, or prejudice."[9]

If we look at the Greek definition, *sober* conveys a calm and collected spirit and to be temperate, dispassionate, or circumspect. Also, it means to be discreet (figuratively) and to literally watch. When translated into Greek, *sober* is also used to explain someone with a good sense, good judgment, and wisdom, who is levelheaded in times of stress.

Sobriety is about what's gained as well as omitted.

Then there's the term *sober-minded*, referring to a state of mind that is not under the control of a reckless outside force.

More broadly, being sober-minded means that we do not allow ourselves to be captivated by any type of influence that would lead us away from sound judgment. The sober-minded individual is not "intoxicated," figuratively speaking, and is therefore calm under pressure, self-controlled in all areas, and rational.

Being sober and being vigilant are closely connected. The call to be sober is found in multiple places in Scripture (1 Thessalonians 5:6–8; 2 Timothy 4:5; Titus 2:2, 6; 1

Peter 4:7) as is the call to be vigilant or alert (Mark 13:33; Ephesians 6:18; 1 Peter 1:13). To be sober means not to allow ourselves to be influenced by anything that leads us away from God's truth and sound judgment. Therefore, sobriety is a state of being. *Vigilant* means "alertly watchful especially to avoid danger." Vigilance requires action. A vigilant person actively pays attention to what is vying for their attention and what affects their heart and mind. To be sober, then, is to keep a clear mind as we vigilantly keep watch over our lives and the world around us.

To me, sobriety is more than abstinence. It is a physical and emotional lifestyle. Emotional sobriety is living all in by showing up for your life, especially when you'd rather numb, soothe, or avoid your feelings. Physical sobriety is more than not drinking, using, or participating in addictive things. It is choosing a lifestyle that respects self-care and wellness. Sobriety is about what's gained as well as omitted.

Sobriety fuels us to live an even more fulfilling life without the complication of intoxication. My sober journey taught me that life is most exciting when lived all in, embracing instead of numbing feelings or ignoring circumstances. I know from multiple experiences that God consistently provides the specific level of strength I need to push forward in all circumstances. It's a supernatural strength and peace that surpasses my understanding and continually blows my mind—and one I would not have access to if I were not sober and alert enough to receive it. I trust I will weather storms, not on my own merit but because I trust God who has unwaveringly carried me through the hard stuff when I showed up instead of checking out.

Exercise

What is your definition of sober?

_____

_____

_____

What do you want to be free from?
To answer that question, answer these questions: *If you fell asleep, woke up, and your problems were solved, what would be different? What would you notice? Is some substance, habit, or hang-up gone? Name it:*

_____

_____

_____

List the behaviors you want your future self to have.

_____

_____

_____

List the behaviors that you currently have.

_____

_____

_____

Ask yourself:
What discomfort am I choosing to soothe or numb?

_____

_____

_____

_____

How has soothing or numbing this served me?

_____

_____

_____

What has soothing or numbing my discomfort cost me?

_____

_____

_____

What has it cost those I love?

_____

_____

_____

What will it cost my future if I continue to soothe or numb this?

_____

_____

_____

What is the cost of choosing to feel life instead of numbness?

_____

_____

_____

Is this greater or less than the cost of continuing to numb?

_____

_____

What will I gain when I lay down my numbing patterns in order to show up for my life?

_____

_____

_____

_____

How will this benefit my loved ones?

_____

_____

_____

_____

What would my life be like if I changed this now?

_____

_____

_____

_____

How does this make me feel?

_____

_____

_____

Now consider this important question and the follow-up:
Because the obsession I want to leave behind drains me of strength and joy, what lifestyle choices bring me the most strength and joy?

_____

_____

_____

10

*How will I make the lifestyle choices I named my
new ritual?*

_____

_____

_____

By answering these questions, you can get to the heart
of what has been distracting you and focus on what you
want. Then you get to decide how to show up for your
life—and the people you want to surround yourself with
to help you live it.

In Summary

Let's tie a bow on our first section about addiction: There
are things you can and are wise to control such as your
beliefs, thoughts, feelings, and narratives. Ritualistic
soothers, however, offer only an illusion of control. Things
such as alcohol, food, tobacco, drugs, and screen time may
meet your needs temporarily. They may even help you
survive for a season or reason as they quietly become an
addiction.

Addictions are not a moral issue. If you are addicted
to something it is because you acquired a soothing ritual
to meet one or more of your basic human needs at a high
level. Most of us didn't set out to adopt an addiction. Be it
days, weeks, or years—in time innocent intentions turned
to physical dependency.

Examples of dangerous addictions are:
- Alcohol
- Food/Sugar
- Binging/Purging

- Tobacco
- Screens (smartphones, tablets, and so forth)
- Prescription and Illegal Drugs
- Marijuana
- Gambling
- Shopping
- Self-injury (picking, cutting, scratching, and biting)
- _____
- _____

Examples of common addiction accompaniers:
- Rigid Thinking/Perfectionism
- High Sensitivity
- Approval Junkiness
- Comparison
- Control
- Apologizing
- People Pleasing
- Avoiding Conflict
- Self-Soothing
- _____
- _____

List some helpful soothers that you could substitute for harmful ones:

Chapter 5

Two (or More) Sides to Every Story

*Everything can be taken from a man but
one thing: the last of the human freedoms—
to choose one's attitude in any given set of
circumstances, to choose one's own way.*[11]
—VIKTOR FRANKL, HOLOCAUST SURVIVOR

WE'VE DISCUSSED WHAT WE CANNOT CONTROL, such as other people and many life events and circumstances. Now let's discuss what we do have control over—our beliefs and the meanings we attach to our circumstances (also called our narrative or story).

In the past I did not know how to take charge of what I believed about things. My thoughts, feelings, and reactions swayed whichever direction the influential wind was blowing. It seemed reasonable to me that if one of my kids was sad, I would feel down. Or if those around me felt sorry for themselves for missing out during the COVID-19 shutdown, I should commiserate too. If I experienced trauma, I felt sad then stuck. I knew to name the feeling I was experiencing, but I didn't know how not to make that feeling my emotional home. I mistook a feeling for a fact.

> **You get to choose whether you tell a story that exhausts you or one that energizes you.**

Now I know I control the stories I fasten to facts. I can't change all my circumstances and truths. I can choose the meanings and create the narratives I attach to them. A mentor coach I worked with in school showed me how to separate facts from the stories I solder to them in a simple way that I now get to teach my clients and you.

A belief is composed of the truth and what is made up. In other words, the facts and the meaning you attach to those facts mesh over time to form a belief.

In my case, the fact was, I was addicted to alcohol. The story I made up was that I was an undisciplined, weak monster of a human because I couldn't kick my addiction on my own. My belief that I was a monster kept me stuck in a destructive cycle—I believed I was a monster, so I behaved like a monster by continuing to drink even though I hated alcohol and its effects on me. Learning my addiction was not my fault destroyed the belief that I was weak and undisciplined and energized me to move into the solution with help from others.

While the truth remained—I was addicted—my monster narrative changed. I went from addicted monster to addicted woman deserving of sobriety and worthy of a solution through support from others. That change happened in the instant I changed my belief.

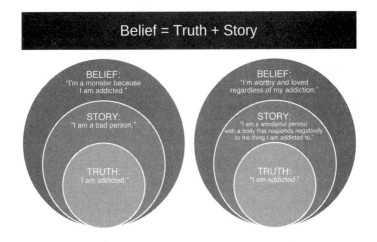

Belief = Truth + Story

BELIEF: "I'm a monster because I am addicted."

STORY: "I am a bad person."

TRUTH: "I am addicted."

BELIEF: "I'm worthy and loved regardless of my addiction."

STORY: "I am a wonderful person with a body that responds negatively to the thing I am addicted to."

TRUTH: "I am addicted."

Here's a visual to explain. The truths are the same yet look at the two beliefs—there's a huge difference. We do not have control over all our truths. We do have control over the stories we attach to them, and those stories determine our beliefs.

The story you tell yourself about something becomes your belief about that thing. That belief can propel you forward or hold you back. You get to choose whether you tell a story that exhausts you or one that energizes you. And that story will cast shadows or light on your past, define your present, and steer your future.

You cannot control all your circumstances; you can control the meanings you choose to attach to them.

You're in charge of what you think about things! You're fully responsible for the stories you attach to the facts in your life.

Again, a belief is made up of two things: what's true plus what's made up. Truth plus story. It's that simple.

So, is your story exhausting or energizing? An exhausting story is spawned when the factual and the fabricated mangle together over time to create an unsound, destructive belief. You can live for years believing an exhausting story. That story may even feel comfortable and safe because you've formed identity or significance in that old tale. For me, the story that I was a monster because I was addicted became an identity I wore like a warm coat, putting it on over and over again every time a craving hit.

On the flip side, an energizing story develops when the truth about an event interweaves with your positive interpretation of that truth to create a sound, constructive belief. Once I changed my story, I substituted the warm coat with the comfort of my support group. Attending regularly and connecting with others like me invigorated a new identity and substituted a positive soother for a harmful one.

You cannot control all your circumstances; you can control the meanings you choose to attach to them. Use this jump-start exercise to gain clarity on the stories you tell yourself.

Exercise

Think of a circumstance that led to an unwanted feeling for you. What meaning did you attach to that circumstance?

_____

_____

_____

_____

Was it an empowering interpretation of the event or a disempowering interpretation?

_____

_____

_____

_____

If disempowering, was your interpretation of the event true or something you unintentionally fabricated?

_____

_____

_____

_____

What would have been a better interpretation?

_____

_____

_____

_____

Now think of a circumstance that led to a feeling you desired.

_____

_____

_____

_____

What meaning did you attach to that circumstance?

_____

_____

_____

*Was it an empowering interpretation of the event or
a disempowering interpretation?* (My guess is it was
empowering.)

_____

_____

_____

_____

See the difference? Controlling the meaning you
attach to circumstances is a life-changing brain shift.
Disempowering meanings are narratives that cause
despair. When natural pain happens (and it will), you get
to choose if you allow the pain to crush you or roll over
you like a wave. Sure, the rolling takes time, and it hurts.
And a supportive story helps create perseverance and
grit for the next painful wave.

Exercise

Change Your Story

Owning an energizing story that serves you well requires identifying and destroying the exhausting story (or stories) you've been telling yourself for days, weeks, months, or maybe years.

This exercise will help you understand how to identify your old story and create a new one.

Step One: Using a sheet of paper marked with two columns, write your story in the left column exactly as you hear it going through your mind. Write your name at the top of the page, designating it as your story.

Step Two: To energize the rewrite of your story, separate what's true from what's fabricated about yourself by circling only the factual points in your left column. The facts you circle are part of your new story. Some truths will be circumstances outside of your control. Ask yourself, *If I were committed to finding an empowering meaning to attach to this truth, what would that be?*

Step Three: In the right column, write your new, energizing story as you want it to be, beginning with the true points you circled in the left column, noting truths and new meanings.

Use the present tense and positive language. Avoid words such as *don't* (substitute *I want* or *I am*), *but* (substitute *and*), and *I have to, I need to, I should* (substitute *I want to, I get to, I choose to*). Positive language—what you write, say to yourself, or voice aloud—will train your mind to tell stories that serve you. With conditioning, powerful storytelling will become natural for you.

Step Four: Cut the columned paper in half to separate the left side (old story) and right side (new story). Now you have visual representations of your exhausting old narrative and your energizing new one.

Here's the fun part: Destroy your exhausting story! Tear it up. Burn it. Boil it. Flush it. Do whatever is meaningful for you to send it to its final resting place. Make this powerful and memorable, mentally and physically. Say aloud with conviction, "I commit to letting my old story go!"

To make the destruction of your old story even more impactful, tell a trusted friend what you did and send that individual a picture of how you destroyed it. Or invite that person to the demolition celebration!

Another impactful idea to add to this exercise is to put heavy things, such as books, cans, or rocks, into a backpack. Wear the heavy backpack for a bit before you destroy your old story. Immediately after you trash it, put down the backpack. This exercise trains your nervous system to remember that your old story was a heavy burden. The new one is light and invigorating! Get creative in associating pain with the old account and pleasure with the new one in whatever clever way is meaningful for you.

It's OK if you don't believe your new story just yet. Be patient with yourself and realize it took time to form the old story, so it may take time to embrace your new one. Writing it down as you want it to be creates both a brain print and a heart print. With time and conditioning, you'll build trust in your new story.

Get creative with how to condition yourself with the new story. Declare it. Make it an affirmation. Speak it aloud. Use body motions. Post it where you can see it every day. Recite its truths at least twice daily to meld them into your physiology and create new neural pathways in your brain.

Beliefs are just your version of what's happened. And you get to choose what you tell yourself!

You have the power to utilize what life brings you instead of being used by it. As the sole narrator of your story, own it! Tell a powerful story that emboldens and energizes you![12]

Fill in your own belief assessment to choose the meaning you attach to your truth:

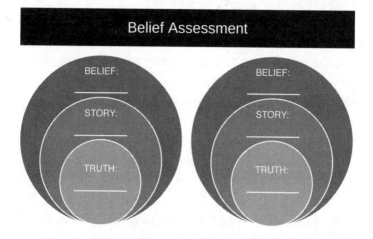

Belief Assessment

BELIEF:

STORY:

TRUTH:

BELIEF:

STORY:

TRUTH:

If you're dissatisfied with what you believe or how you feel about what you believe, remember, beliefs are just your version of what's happened. And you get to choose what you tell yourself!

Chapter 6

Allergy

*And I know we can't fix every ache inside of us. But
I shouldn't have to pretend it's not there either.*

—COLIN, *TED LASSO*

Remember the woman at my first support group meeting who said the words that sent decades of shame lifting off my shoulders? "It is not your fault. You are alcoholic. It is like an allergy." The words not only removed my shame but launched my curiosity for how alcohol shows up in my body and why I have a different reaction to it than other people.

What works for me is a belief that alcohol is like an allergy. I'm not saying it *is* an allergy. I am not a doctor. I believe alcohol is *like* an allergy. Here's why. Having an allergy means I have an abnormal response to something in my system. Knowing this about myself protects me.

My youngest son, Jake, has been allergic to peanuts and tree nuts his entire life. The allergy doctor explained it to Scott and me when Jake was a child as: "Jake may ingest a nut and experience no consequences. He may ingest a nut and have a mild to severe sensitivity. Or he may ingest a nut, go into anaphylactic shock, and die. He must stay away from nuts because science today cannot tell us what his response will be. Until we know otherwise, Jake must treat nuts as a deadly threat and abstain from them altogether."

The doctor prescribed an EpiPen. It was my son's protection in the case of exposure to nuts leading to anaphylactic shock. The pen will not save Jake's life; however, the epinephrine it injects will buy him twenty minutes until an ambulance arrives or he gets to a hospital. The only sure protection against death by nuts is to avoid accidental or intentional ingestion of them.

When Jake was in kindergarten, I got a call to come down to the school because he'd encountered a nut. It was a birthday celebration for a classmate whose mom brought snacks that day—granola with nuts. Although precautions had been taken to have Jake sit at the end of the table with his own snack I'd packed, his five-year-old fingers managed to make their way toward a neighbor who shared their granola with Jake. Jake told his teacher his hands and throat were itchy, and in minutes the school nurse administered his EpiPen and called 911. By the time I got to the school, paramedics had Jake buckled on a stretcher and were starting to wheel him down the corridor toward the ambulance. Mrs. B., our family's beloved kindergarten teacher then on her third Janssen kid, was bent over the stretcher, following as it moved. Her arms were outstretched over Jake's small body as she prayed over him out loud (it was a Christian school). Jake looked fine. He was not in shock, physically or emotionally, and said "Hi, Mommy" as he clutched a teddy bear from the paramedics. I don't know how Jake's reaction to the nut would have escalated had he not been in proximity to a community invested in his survival, both with quick actions and vehement prayer. I'm grateful I didn't have to find out. I followed the ambulance to the hospital where they spent the next few hours monitoring Jake; then we got to go home, healthy and stable.

Jake is twenty-two years old now and has not outgrown his nut allergy. A few more accidental run-ins with hidden nuts in foods and sauces over the years have proved that. His reactions have varied from severe stomach pain, to vomiting, to an itchy throat. In all cases Jake got help from his EpiPen or visiting an ER before it escalated to a life-threatening level. While adult Jake is vigilant enough to stay clear of nuts, he is also vigilant to still carry an EpiPen—lest a nut creep up on him.

My sober community is my EpiPen. The group alone cannot save my life—only abstinence from alcohol can do that. But the group buys me time, one day at a time. It would be silly to abstain from alcohol without the protection of the group, just as it would be silly for Jake not to carry an EpiPen with him. Although Jake does not intend to eat nuts, he lives in a world where nuts and nut-laced foods abound. Like nuts, the threat of alcohol lurks at every meal and social gathering and requires physical and mental vigilance, a supportive community, and at least one Mrs. B. in our corner!

Alcoholic like Me

I've heard current influencers and authors in the sober space say that the words *sobriety* and *recovery* have a bad branding, are negative, or don't make someone want to get sober. One author, when asked about their sobriety date, responded, "I drink as much as I want whenever I want. I just haven't wanted to drink in ___ years now." I've heard others respond with, "I can drink alcohol if I want; I just choose not to today." That thought process is working for them and their followers.

However, that does not work for me, because what happens if one day I *do* want to drink? That thinking places a ton of trust on the individual not to want to drink. I don't trust my human ability to control every want, whim, or whisper of temptation in the moment. Believing I can choose to drink whenever I want is tricky thinking, since I don't know when and if my allergic response to alcohol will kick in. Also, to me, the words *recovery* and *sobriety* are vibrant and invigorating. Synonyms for *recovery* include *regain, recapture, reclaim, get back, redeem, recoup, renew, revive,* and *rally.*

This is one reason knowing *why* you fell into an addiction and *why* you want out of it are important. Why do you want to reclaim you? Why are you committing to a sober lifestyle? Conviction and commitment are decisions. Desire is a feeling. I can trust I'll act on my decisions, but not always my feelings. We'll discuss your *why* in the next chapter. You are wired uniquely and must commit to emotional and physical sobriety for yourself, because what works for one person to get and stay sober may not work for another person, and assuming it does can be damaging. For me, reading the previously mentioned thought leaders' suggestions for how to look at addiction and alcohol tripped me up.

Synonyms for recovery include *regain, recapture, reclaim, get back, redeem, recoup, renew, revive,* and *rally.*

Some sober influencers also discourage calling oneself "alcoholic." The idea is that it is a punitive, stigmatic label. I'm for *all* sobriety movements. Sobriety is a win. I'm not supportive of some of the methods of the movements, however, like discouraging labels such as "alcoholic" that are already working for millions of people. While recent mindful drinking or sober-curious movements work for some people either to drink less or abstain from alcohol, some of the language used by these influencers and authors can leave those of us vulnerable who have been and are being helped by the "alcoholic" label.

Of course, limiting or abstaining from drinking alcohol is wise, just as abstaining from drinking gasoline is wise. Both are crummy wellness choices. Cheers to the people the movements are helping. I have some normie clients who are benefiting by moving to a lifestyle of drinking less or no alcohol. They are not like me, though. They are not allergic like I am. They are not alcoholic like me.

My snag with people influencing the sober space by preaching that no one is alcoholic, and the reason we can't or shouldn't use alcohol is simply because it is a poisonous drug, is that this information is only half true. Some of us have an abnormal response to alcohol and are wired differently than normies (those who do not have an abnormal response to alcohol). While alcohol is a drug, there are some people who can limit their alcohol. I knew several family members on Scott's side who lived an entire lifetime moderating alcohol and then died of old age without ever getting themselves on the alcohol use disorder (AUD) spectrum. It happens. That doesn't mean alcohol isn't poisonous or addictive. It just means it doesn't derail everybody the way it damaged me and those like me.

Moderation is messy for me but not for everybody. Not everybody has used the substance in enough quantity or frequency to become addicted to it, and we all differ in what quantity and frequency it takes to become addicted. So books and content that lump all humans into the same category are dicey and almost took me out.

When I broke my sobriety to test my alcoholism, I read much of the fresh content I'm referring to and believed the myths that (1) I'm not alcoholic and (2) I can simply choose to drink or not. One book lays out the scientific facts about alcohol's toxicity, and the hope is that by the end of the book you'll be so disgusted that you won't want to drink it. As a result, many readers choose to limit alcohol then abstain completely—which should be the first clue that the readers for which this approach works are not ensnared by their addiction.

Here is what I mean: Addiction will get what it wants—no matter what! Addiction leaves no room for reasoning with the substance by weighing its health benefits and downfalls. Addiction will choose the substance over loved ones, higher powers, and personal standards. Addiction will make a person break every rule or premise they live by in every other area of their life. You can be the healthiest friend, spouse, parent, leader, or worshipper, yet when it comes to the thing you're addicted to, all bets are off, the rules don't apply, and every pattern in every other area of your life is meaningless. That is addiction.

It's not that I think the recent books shouldn't be taught. I think they should come with a warning: "This is a book about healthy lifestyle and not meant for the person in an active addiction." That way the books can help people, like some of my normie clients or family members, by providing evidence for why drinking is damaging to the health of all humans.

For me, reading those books while I was unsuccessfully attempting to moderate alcohol was a green light—because I was trapped in an active addiction, and that addiction running amok in me at that time tirelessly ignored science presented to me regarding dopamine, neuroplasticity, alcohol toxicity, or how long it takes for alcohol to leave my system. All I heard was: *You are not an alcoholic and you can drink if you want to.* I did not care that the sentence went on to explain, however, that I'd choose not to drink after hearing the empirical evidence against alcohol that the book would go on to cover. Addiction doesn't care about evidence.

Addiction craves a hit, not science, and will absorb, refute, or ignore facts that don't serve its purpose, to satisfy that hit.

I was an alcoholic loose in a world of normies, buying the lie that we are all the same and that "limiting my intake" should be just as easy for me as it is for the normie next door (literally —I live in a very social neighborhood, and we love to plan parties). I was in another high-standard, rigid-thinking, lose-lose scenario.

Addiction craves a hit, not science, and will absorb, refute, or ignore facts that don't serve its purpose to satisfy that hit. Let's contrast the recent thought leaders' teachings with the statement that got me sober at my first support meeting in 2007:

1. Recent thought leaders in the sober space are teaching that: *There are not alcoholics and normies (or them and us). Alcohol is bad for everybody, so stop calling yourself an alcoholic. You can drink if you want to, but you won't want to once we provide the science of why alcohol is a harmful drug.*

2. The opposite statement that got me sober at my first support meeting was: *It's not your fault; you*

are alcoholic. It's like an allergy, and you never have to have another drink again.

The second saved my life. The first almost killed me. The reason the new thought leaders' teachings almost killed me is because, after breaking sobriety and during my drinking-curious experiment, reading information like this led me to believe I was not alcoholic and I could drink if I wanted to, which theoretically wouldn't be a problem because I wouldn't want to anymore (according to these new teachers). The problem happened on the days I did want to. What then? I don't eat much sugar. I probably eat cookies three or four times a year, depending on the year. So for the most part, I don't eat cookies because I don't want to. I feel lousy when I eat cookies and I detest feeling lousy. I like feeling good and I know what simple carbs do to my brain, blood sugar, and energy, which make me not want a cookie—most of the time. There are a few times, however, I want a cookie, and at those times I eat the cookie. I cannot do this with alcohol. A cookie won't kill me. Alcohol might. Alcohol may not harm all subscribers to that logic. Since it will harm me, though, I do not subscribe to that logic.

Addiction will do what it wants—*no matter what.* It must be responded to in its own language, and to me that looks like, *I do not drink alcohol—no matter what.* Not because I don't want to but because it will trigger my allergy—my abnormal response to alcohol. That response goes like this:

- My first sip ignites an instant feeling of euphoria;
- which fires up an immediate obsession to keep that feeling going;

- which flares up a frenzy for more alcohol;
- which kindles a focus group with the voices in my head to strategize how to get more alcohol;
- which rouses my success in getting more alcohol (because I'm an achiever who conquers her goals);
- which riles up drunkenness;
- which stimulates more strategizing to get more alcohol, this time in a drunken state;
- which provokes hiding, sneaking, lying, and using insane judgment (things the sober me does not entertain) to achieve my goal;
- which fans further success of reaching the goal;
- which breaks out into getting even drunker;
- which engages vomiting and blacking out;
- which intensifies confusion and erases memories;
- which fuels passing out;
- which erupts in waking up having to hear about how Scott kept me alive by getting my head out of the toilet water or turning the bath water off, washing me off, and putting me to bed;
- which worsens guilt (for what I did) and shame (for who I am);
- which inflames a hangover and a wasted day;
- which exacerbates not being able to cope with the physical sickness, the hangxiety, and the craving for another hit to make it all go away;
- which ignites taking another "first sip" as a remedy and soother.

A popular saying in recovery is, "The definition of insanity is doing the same thing over and over again and expecting a different result." Being caught in an addictive loop, like the one I just described, is insanity.

Like Jake taking his doctor's advice and treating nuts as a threat to death, I now treat alcohol as a deadly threat. Yes, there were times when I pulled it off. I drank alcohol without igniting the vomiting and blacking out. There were occasions during my drinking-curious experiment when the focus group in my head got it right and shut down the strategizing for more alcohol before it started. I got lucky on those occasions.

I wanted to outsmart the insanity until, thankfully, the insanity outsmarted me.

For me, one time almost drowning in vomit or bathwater should have been enough to quit testing my luck. Unfortunately, it wasn't. And the harder I worked at replaying the few times I drank without blacking out, the more I exacerbated my allergy. I wanted to outsmart the insanity until, thankfully, the insanity outsmarted me.

Like the doctor advised Jake, since I don't know what my reaction will be, I must treat alcohol as a threat to death and abstain from it altogether. I've proven again and again that I qualify as a person with an abnormal response to alcohol, but I wanted so badly to use my few dignified drinking examples as evidence that I am the normie next door.

I no longer recall those episodes with false hope that I have outgrown my allergy to alcohol, because I have exited the insanity loop.

Being out of the loop means remembering my last drunk episode with lucid gratitude for my alcohol-free life and the freedom I now have.

Chapter 7

The Why

100% is easier than 98%.
—Dr. Benjamin Hardy

IF YOUR COMMITMENT TO ABSTINENCE IS CONDI-
tional, your brain will create a condition to justify
breaking that commitment. If your commitment to
abstinence is unconditional, your brain won't entertain a
loophole.

For me, a loophole is free rein. One gift my drinking-
curious experiment gave me was that Scott is now
convinced that, for me, one sip will lead to trouble. During
my first round of sobriety he, like me, was 90 percent
certain I could not drink. There was a small part that was
not certain, though. So when I consulted with him about
picking up a drink again, he, like me, did not see the harm
in it. We both forgot over time what a nasty response I
have to alcohol. We didn't realize that while I had evolved,
my reaction to alcohol had not.

One bonus of gaining my sobriety back a second time
is that now Scott and I are both 100 percent convinced I
cannot drink. We both know I will not survive another
"going out." Here's the thing though—what Scott is
convinced or not convinced of does not matter. What
matters is that I know that, for me, to drink is to flirt with
death. If you are addicted and looking for reassurance
from another person to validate your addiction or hold
you accountable for your recovery, you are in a dangerous
situation. You are the only one who can decide to get or
stay sober.

By going out and returning to sobriety, I've realized
that the first time I discovered sobriety, though I believed
I was sober, I was alcohol-free to hold everything together.
I had a marriage, three small kids, pets, a house, extended
family dynamics, and a reputation to manage. I was a

Bible study facilitator and Parent Teacher Association president, for heaven's sake. Being sober for all these reasons, while healthy, was not sustainable. Since my *why* for not drinking had been to hold things together, the very month my youngest kid left for college and we moved to a different state for a fresh start, and all the things I'd been responsible for holding were suddenly able to hold themselves, I, for the first time in thirteen years, craved a martini.

Though I believed otherwise, I had not been sober for myself as I am now. I know now that no matter what is happening around me, no matter what I oversee, and no matter who suggests I am capable of being a normal drinker—for me, to drink is to play with fire. I cannot drink—no matter what.

If your commitment to abstinence is conditional, your brain will create a condition to justify breaking that commitment.

Why do you want to be free of the thing you want to get free from, and who are you doing it for? Is it for health reasons? Your kids? Your partner, parents, or others? Is it to be perceived in a different light? For your reputation? For more productivity? For better athletic performance? Because it's Dry January or Sober October? There is no right or wrong answer here. What matters is that you know, without a doubt, *why* you want to get free.

If you don't know why you want something, when the temptation to do the thing you think you don't want to do hits, your brain will rationalize a reason why it makes sense to do it. This is not you. It's your brain. You are not weak-willed. You have a human brain like everybody else. Replace guilt over acquiescing with curiosity for *why* you decided not to partake in that thing in the first place.

Guilt will only distract you from getting where you want to go. Ditch it and write down why you want what you want. Believe in your why. Recite it as an affirmation or mantra daily. Your mind will get creative and test your why. You are smart and it would be weird if your mind didn't spin a story against your solid lifestyle decision. Your brilliant brain is wired to question your beliefs and choices. Let it. Then be prepared to answer those questions with choices and beliefs that serve you and move you in the direction you want to go. Once your why is set and you believe in it, it becomes your fortress and ammunition once the arrows of the mind start flying. The arrows will come. It's not wrong; it's wiring.

The second time I worked to get sober, I did not write down my why for wanting an alcohol-free lifestyle at first, so freedom from the obsession of alcohol took a while to take hold. My brain and body's pattern (we all have patterns, whether we're aware of them or not) was to go a few months happy to be alcohol-free, then hit a wall of boredom. I would think, *Why did I give up alcohol again?* So I would drink and be quickly reminded—until I forgot again. My "forgetter" needed fixing, and that started with getting clear on my reasons for wanting an alcohol-free life.

Now I have a solid *why* to believe in when the flimsy negotiations in my mind begin to fly. In addition to almost killing me, alcohol scrambled my hormones, blood sugar, and frame of mind—necessities I work daily to energize. Ingesting alcohol made me more sad than happy. It made me have less fun—and I love fun.

Now when the temptation comes in the form of logical questions asked by a sexy siren, I celebrate my brain, thank it for being ever so clever, then respond with a *Thanks, but no thanks. How about you work it out on the dance floor while I enjoy the VIP lounge.* Give it a whirl. During that time visit your why and your commitment and remind yourself of the reward waiting for you when the siren stops singing. The waters will calm, and you'll reach the shore.

For me the shore of a sober life cannot be measured against what drinking provided me. Drinking only ever gave me

Remind yourself of the reward waiting for you when the siren stops singing. The waters will calm, and you'll reach the shore.

something to do in a moment. Sobriety gives me a lifetime of experiences and memories. In sobriety I write, I run, I belly laugh, I weep, I have extra time in my day, I love well, I grieve well, I remember things richly, and I experience feelings, sounds, smells, and sights in ways I never did during a drinking season because all my sensory receptors and brain cells were consumed with the act of drinking and where the next drink would come from.

When we remove the obsession for alcohol, life lights us up with everything else! Every smile, heartache, hug, and celebration can be felt intensely in sobriety, and it's all good. The feelings—all of them—are what being alive and living all in is all about.

Chapter 8

Vigilance and Fear

There is no fear in love. But perfect love drives out fear, because fear has to do with punishment. The one who fears is not made perfect in love.
—1 John 4:18

W E TALKED ABOUT REASONS FOR GETTING FREE in the last chapter. Fear is a common motivator for people getting sober. Sometimes it's a loved one's fear for us that pushes us to get help. Maybe it's fear for ourself and what could go wrong. While fear is a powerful motivator, so is love. In this chapter, I'll discuss how to lead from love and vigilance instead of fear.

Have you ever tossed a fear repeatedly in your mind until it became a harsh reality? What about the opposite? Have you focused so intently on achieving something fabulous that you made it happen? Chances are you got what you wanted when you created a trust-centered temperament and listened to your heart instead of your head—when you led your life with invigorating love, not debilitating fear.

Maybe you've been on the flip side of fear-based leadership when a parent or authority figure led from fears of what you may or may not do instead of trusting in what you're capable of doing. How did that fear-based leadership make you feel? Did you live down to those poor expectations and fears? Or did you use them as fuel to rise above and thrive?

You get the result you anticipate—desired or undesired—so leading out of fear is debilitating, in parenting, business, finances, performance, life, *and sobriety.*

As leaders and loved ones, we do not hold the power to scare others into sobriety or a life we think they should live. I want my sobriety to be motivated by my love of freedom—not by fear. My recovery must be rooted in acceptance of God's grace for me and trust that my future sobriety, while not assured, is attainable. I must live with anticipation of my sober life instead of fear of picking up a drink. A key distinction here is being vigilant is different from fear. Vigilance is being alert and watchful in order to protect your sobriety by having a plan when lurking temptations arise. Fear is anticipating those temptations will take you down. First Peter 5:8 says, "Be alert and of sober mind. Your enemy the devil prowls around like a roaring lion looking for someone to devour." Be alert, not afraid.

The first time I got sober I believed it was for me; however, upon reflection, I realized it was for fear of failing my kids and Scott. It was to hold everything and everyone together. I know this because once the kids were grown and flown, I believed my job was done. I believed I could relax and have a drink—so I did. My decision to pick up a drink after several years of continuous sobriety was a decision made from curiosity, not weakness. I broke my sobriety from a high point in my life, not a low one. Though the result was not what I wanted or imagined, I learned that being vigilant is necessary in the high times as well as the low times. Temptation will come for us in our highest and lowest moments. Addiction is a beast. Addiction doesn't care if we're in a pit or on a mountaintop. It will find us if we are not alert.

> **Being vigilant is different from fear. Vigilance is being alert and watchful in order to protect your sobriety by having a plan when lurking temptations arise. Fear is anticipating those temptations will take you down.**

I get what I focus on. I get what I want. I've been trained as a coach to focus on what I want instead of what I want to avoid (because I'll get that too), and I work with clients to do the same. One thing that led to me breaking my continuous sobriety is that I wanted to be a normie. I wanted to drink "on occasion." I did not pick up a drink after thirteen-plus years out of weakness. I picked it up deliberately—to test the "alcoholism as an allergy" idea. I decided to see for myself if alcoholism is a progressive condition. The experiment was deliberate. While I don't recommend it, it was a decision made from intelligent curiosity, not failed willpower.

This is where being alert is crucial. Our intelligence can really spin some doozies, can't it? I thought my way into a drinking-curious experiment because I was in a new town and didn't have my familiar sober community to remind me that alcoholism is a progressive condition and is like an allergy—and I have not magically outgrown it. Smart me had to relearn that for herself.

You, too, get what you focus on. You picked up your habit of choice on purpose. You partook because you decided to. Once you choose sobriety you never have to pick up that thing you were addicted to again—unless you decide to. To be clear, *deciding* is different from wanting, craving, or being tempted to do something. The first is a choice. The second is a feeling. I mentioned earlier how sober thought leaders' statements such as, "I can drink as much as I want whenever I want; I just haven't wanted to in __ years now," confused and then influenced me. The distinction between commitment and desire is clear to me now. *Deciding* to create a penetrable loophole is different from *wanting* to. You can decide to take that first sip or not. You can commit to not taking a first sip no matter what. You cannot decide or predict whether you'll desire to take that first sip if a craving hits.

Commit to not taking a first sip and grace yourself if you crave one. A craving is not wrong. It's human. You do not need to satisfy your craving, though! We live in a self-help culture that preaches gratification, balance, and moderation. Where does that leave those of us who cannot moderate? Are we the weak ones who can't keep up? No! Here is your permission to abstain. It is OK to deny yourself things you see others enjoying effortlessly. In time you'll learn you are not denying yourself pleasure by saying no to a drink because a sober life will become the greater pleasure. Until that shift happens, know that the people able to enjoy alcohol are not stronger than you. They simply are not allergic to the same things you are. There is nothing weird about you if you cannot tolerate alcohol. Trying to "enjoy" something that will make you sick just because you see others enjoying it will not bring the pleasure you think it will.

It's important to note that I'm using "first sip" because, for the alcoholic like me, the first sip turns us into a person who wants more sips. It ignites the obsession for more. I have zero tips for how to limit alcohol intake after the first sip, because I have not accomplished that. Even when I did pull off not getting drunk or avoided having a second or third drink, I have never pulled off not obsessing over the idea of it. What I know is, before the first sip I have everything I need intellectually and physically to say no to a first hit, even if I'm craving it. No one is twisting my arm except my own cravings, and I am smarter than my cravings. Let your commitment and conviction to what you decided ahead of time (before the craving hit) be your guide. A craving is just a feeling. It does not have the final say.

If you are a parent, it's like this: You brought a baby into your home one day and committed to raising and caring for them. You committed to your child's survival. The child is not perfect. It cries, it's hungry, it grows into a rebellious teen, and so on. Even though you may feel like it on some days, you do not return your child to the local hospital or fire station doorstep. There will be days you crave vacation, or alone time, or space when those things are not possible because of your commitment to your child. That is the difference between commitment and craving. There is a distinction between decision and desire.

You do not need to live down to other people's weak fears for you. You decide. You choose. While there are no guarantees in recovery, there are choices. You are 100 percent responsible for your own choices as much as you are not 1 percent responsible for the choices, fears, and opinions of others. They have a right to be fearful for you, and you have a right to decide how those fears land on you. Like rain droplets on a waterproof jacket, allow other people's stuff to bead up and roll off you if it doesn't serve you—and fears don't serve you.

Mind your mind with these tips for creating a trust-centered belief system that works in your favor:

- Trust yourself if advice or pressure to have "just one" doesn't sit well with you. Write down your decisions and why you chose them to enforce your trust in them.

- Believe your loved ones are capable of miraculous things. You hold influence over whether they live up to your extraordinary beliefs in them or down to your greatest fears for them.
- Stop and get curious if something doesn't feel right. Ask yourself if you've bought into a well-meaning leader or loved one's (or your own) misdirected fears for you.
- Purge beliefs that don't serve you, to create space for those that do. Everyone has a right to their opinions, beliefs, and fears, and you have the right to decide how those land on you.
- Discern between fear and vigilance. Fear is expecting the worst. Vigilance is recognizing the worst in order to implement a safety plan.

If you want an alcohol-free life, commit to that. Stay alert so you'll notice cravings when they pop up (and they *will* pop up). Then be vigilant by implementing a plan of action for when cravings arise. Use the following exercise to create a plan for staying vigilant to your commitments.

Exercise

Commitment = Purpose + Plan

Decide what you must commit to in order to become the person you want to become. Write your commitment here:

Next, establish a plan to stay vigilant to your commitments:

Start by establishing your purpose (why your commitment is a must for you):

1. Close your eyes and visualize your desired outcome. Breathe it in. See it. Feel it. Smell it. Hear it. Now, focusing on your visualized outcome as if it is happening right now, ask yourself:
   - *How do I feel?*
   - *What does this mean to me?*
   - *What does this mean to my loved ones?*
   - *Who have I become?*
2. Now anchor this feeling with a physical movement. Snap your fingers, tighten your fist, pump your chest, clap, or perform some motion that you will repeat every time you want to connect to this feeling and your why going forward.
3. Capture your answers on paper. This is your purpose—the emotional charge behind why you want what you want.

As you make progress toward your outcome, practice connecting to your why often. Repetition and conditioning are key to getting where you want to go.

Next, create a plan to get the outcome you've decided to commit to. It's effective to establish your why, or purpose, before you move to your plan, or strategy. Your why is the emotional charge fueling your action plan.

1. To get your plan, repeat step one from the preceding: Close your eyes and visualize your desired outcome. Breathe it in. See it. Feel it. Smell it. Hear it. Now, focusing on your visualized outcome as if it is happening right now, ask yourself:

   - *What specific actions did I take to get to this moment?*

2. Using pen or pencil, capture what comes to mind on paper. Be specific. Write down all the actions you'll take to get your outcome.

3. Then ask yourself, *What else?* Write that down too.

4. Now you have a plan. A strategy.

5. Go through your list of actions, making sure each is specific. If you wrote, "Exercise five days a week," write down the times, days, length, and type of exercise. If you wrote, "Go on a run or walk when a craving hits," write down how you will execute this. Will you keep athletic shoes in your car or at work? If you wrote, "Call a supportive friend when a craving hits," write down names and numbers and keep them in your phone or favorites list. You are in charge of the specifics. Just be sure the actions are specific and details are established to stay ahead of your cravings or temptations.

There is a difference between choice and craving. Cravings will present on their own time. A choice can be predetermined. You cannot control all your wants and cravings. You can control what you've decided ahead of time to do with those wants and cravings. You are not guaranteed to not want to partake in your thing ever again. You can decide ahead of time what you'll do when that want arises.

Chapter 9

Mistaken Misuse

I began to understand that the world is not so scary if, around every significant corner, somebody is waiting to walk with you on the next part of the journey.

—Bono, Surrender: 40 Songs, One Story

HOW DOES IT FEEL NOW THAT YOU'VE BEEN CLEAR on why you want to commit to the person you want to become? Getting clear on why I must abstain from alcohol (my commitment) to become the person I wanted to become was freeing. Knowing the purpose for my decision opened my lifestyle choices up to even more fun. My why for living alcohol-free was (and is):

- I have more fun when I'm enjoying the moment and the people I'm with. Alcohol gets me thinking about past regrets or future game plans for more drinking and takes me out of the present.
- I have more fun with margin in my day for free time. Alcohol takes time (both the drinking and the thinking), which uses up the extra time I enjoy for snacking, playing with our dog, watching a funny show, hanging out with Scott, or walking outside. All work and no play make me fussy (and kind of mean).
- I have more fun at social events when I'm energized. Alcohol overstimulates and exhausts me, which keeps me in my head, not engaged with others, and scheming ways to leave the event early.
- I have more fun when I wake up early. I'm an early riser and love my morning energy. Alcohol robs me of my enjoyable mornings.
- I have more fun when I feel good and my digestion works properly. Alcohol messes with my physical well-being and digestion.
- I have more fun knowing I'm available for unforeseen events, such as Scott or one of the kids needing

me for an emergency or just to talk. Alcohol warps my alertness and patience.

- I have more fun when my blood sugar, nervous system, and hormones are at healthy levels. Alcohol upsets these systems.
- I have more fun when I remember events and can laugh with loved ones about moments shared. Alcohol fades or taints my memories.
- My life is more fun without guilt, shame, or remorse (need I say more?).
- I have more fun when I'm happy. Alcohol makes me feel happy for a little while and then causes feelings of sadness and anxiety for a long while. No fun.
- I have more fun knowing my freedom is sustainable. Alcohol makes me "feel" free—for a moment—then it makes me feel trapped. Alcohol is fleeting fun. I'm into real fun.

Releasing the burden of entertaining drinking decisions freed me to live all in and show up for the life I want. I now know instinctively when information I've ingested does not apply to me because I am clear on why I decided to abstain from alcohol. I want that for you too. Investment in the exercise from the previous chapter will solidify your why and allow you to instinctively know how to choose your commitment over your craving should a desire pop up (and it will).

In addition to becoming confused while reading new content by sober thought leaders during my drinking-curious experiment, I experienced this contradiction in person. One of the actions I attempted to regain my sobriety was to attend a faith-based 12-step group. In true Coach Chris form, I leapt all in and showed up for the program with all of me. I bought the books, committed to the meetings, and did the homework. The program helps people get free from any harmful habit, not just alcohol. The group consisted of people recovering from hang-ups and hurts such as codependency and addictions to food, alcohol, sex, digital screens, and substances.

I heard testimonies of women making strides and getting unstuck from strongholds, so I was hopeful (and eager to jump in and *recover real quick*). As I am big on mentorship, I asked a woman to be my mentor after hearing her speak in the group and during my first week of attendance. Our first time working together, the woman told me that in addition to codependency and another addiction, she had also "recovered from alcohol misuse." I asked her to clarify, and she told me she used to binge drink and now she can stop after one or two drinks. *Whaaaat! This is more fun than I thought it was going to be. This woman is living free, and she is drinking without misusing alcohol? Glory hallelujah, I've found my people! Sign me up for this mindful drinking plan. Give me the manual, let's go.*

She shared her story and how she prayed to be free from all that was binding her, then had a habit-changing spiritual experience. I know God can and does change people. I've experienced God removing strongholds in my own life. I also know, in the past, God has not changed me into someone who can moderate their alcohol intake. Nevertheless, I went home from my mentor meeting and prayed to be "free from alcohol misuse." I wanted my inability to moderate alcohol use to be lifted. It wasn't, but still I had to test to make certain. The night of that mentor meeting, after praying for God to remove my alcohol misuse, I forged ahead as a revolutionized normie and had a drink. Then drinks. Then I blacked out, fell down, threw up, passed out, and woke, twelve hours later, only because Scott watched over me all night. That was the night of my last drink, which I'll come back to. The following day has now become my new sobriety date. I went back to the sober community that saved my life in 2007 and am currently still active within the group. I forged ahead, not down; injected my EpiPen; and recovered my sobriety. I clawed my way up to my people and myself.

I believe that God did help the sincere mentor woman break free from strongholds, including alcohol. She says she is now able to drink one drink without igniting an obsession for more, and I believe her. But she is not like me, does not respond to alcohol like I do, and is not the mentor for me. Seeking counsel to succeed like her at what is impossible for me was wishful mentorship. I wouldn't ask a bird to mentor me in being a bird even though I think being a bird would be super cool, so I can't ask a normie to mentor me in living alcohol-free, even if that normie does abstain from alcohol most of the time. It's not the same.

Again, being clear on your why is a must. Your why is personal. As I said earlier, the program or community that works for one person to gain freedom may or may not work for you. You'll test different methods before you land on what works. The testing is necessary and fruitful.

Keep going until you land where you can expand and encourage others to do the same.

Sometimes rigid thinkers hit pause or quit the search altogether on their way to getting where they want to go—again, because of that annoying tendency to want the ideal. If it's not perfect, we plateau. Instead, tweak the tactics for getting where you want to go. Keep what works and move on from what doesn't. Refinement is happening during your search, and nothing tested is a waste.

There is power in proximity, so surround yourself with those who already have what you want.

Once you find a supportive community that works (we will discuss this further in chapter 12), focus on the similarities you have with the group instead of the differences. A healthy group will include individuals with the same recovery goal as yours, not the same personality.

There is power in proximity, so surround yourself with those who already have what you want. That is influence, not comparison. Influence will push you up. Comparison will tear you down.

Chapter 10

Shame of Stigma

To be passive is to let others decide for you. To be aggressive is to decide for others. To be assertive is to decide for yourself. And to trust that there is enough, that you are enough.
—Edith Eva Eger

ONE CHALLENGE TO CUTTING ALCOHOL OUT OF my life in 2007 was explaining to well-meaning loved ones that, as much as they perceived I was able to control alcohol, I wasn't. I shouldn't have had to explain going alcohol-free to anyone; however, my social circle at that time demanded an explanation—or, more likely, I imagined they did. Believing that people deserved an explanation from me seems silly in hindsight, especially since current society embraces mocktails, wellness, and the alcohol-free lifestyle even for people who aren't pregnant, headed to rehab, or prepping for a medical procedure.

I cared far more about others' perceptions of me in my thirties than I do now in my midfifties. One person close to me consistently had a remark if I answered, "No, thank you," to an alcoholic beverage at their home during cocktail hour or a celebratory occasion, which were frequent. Unless I was pregnant, the message I received in response was that I was rude not to imbibe in one drink. I had not yet developed the tools to realize saying no was an option. And since I couldn't have one without a vampirical frenzy for more taking over, some of my best drunks were at this person's home. It was yet another example of me compromising who I am and what I want in order to manipulate another person's perception of me. Again, people pleasing to make myself feel better was masked as respect for the person offering the drink. True honor of this person would have looked like being steadfast in my personal convictions. I caused far more long-term harm in the relationship than I would have caused short-term disappointment.

The tragic thing is it was another lose-lose. If I took the drink to get approval (or avoid disapproval) and then got drunk—lose. If I said no to the drink because I knew what would happen and I hated getting drunk—lose. The better answer would have been to make the latter (saying no thank you) a win by knowing my why and myself. Allowing people the right to think what they will, knowing my behavior has zip to do with what they decide to think about me, is a win. I did not and do not hold the power to manipulate how others perceive me.

With pregnancy or problem drinker being the only logical reasons a person would say no to a drink, I got clever with my nos. If I wasn't sneaking drinks, I was skirting the truth about why I wasn't drinking. *I have a cold. I have to get up early tomorrow. I had a big night last night. I . . .* Either way I became an expert at the art of hiding until I decided that was not a fun way to live. Since I didn't want to be an expert at sneaking anymore, I explained to others why I was no longer drinking, thus labeling myself a problem drinker in their opinion. (Because why in the world would anyone not drink alcohol unless they had a drinking problem?) The truth is, I *did* have a problem with drinking alcohol. It made me vomit and black out. Alcohol was the problem, though, not me, yet I knew others wouldn't see it that way. The sucky part is that it was my business, and I shouldn't have had to explain myself to others in order to answer *no* when offered a drink. Even though I wasn't the problem—alcohol was— there are people who see those of us who have an abnormal response to alcohol as undisciplined drunks, so however I chose to explain it, there was a stigma attached.

I marched forward as a proclaimed problem drinker, which freed me to stop skirting the truth about why I was saying no to a drink. Once my circle knew I didn't drink, I didn't have to explain anymore. I was free to quit hiding if I admitted I had a problem with alcohol, which also meant being willing to accept the stigma that came along with it.

The Art of Hiding

Early in sobriety I believed my program was anonymous to save me from the embarrassment of admitting my truth. This was a weird belief because I was seeking to escape shameful feelings I had been carrying since childhood. It was like trading one secret for another.

> **If being anonymous empowers you, be anonymous. If loud and proud is your style, do that.**

I came to learn that the reason for anonymity is not about me keeping a shameful secret. Anonymity prevents me from blabbing about who else I see in recovery meetings. It also protects the integrity of the group regardless of my actions outside of the group. Twelve-step meetings close with the chairperson reading, "Who you see here, let it stay here." Then the group responds with, "here, here." It is a guideline set in place out of respect—not shame. I am free to recover out loud if I want to (which is what I am doing here). But I do not have the right to decide for others how they recover. Recovery done in community works because the community respects everyone's personal recovery. What works for me will not be what works for others, and understanding this is what works for the group.

If being anonymous empowers you, be anonymous. If loud and proud is your style, do that. Your discovery is yours alone. Do what works for you, not others. There is no right or wrong beyond what works or doesn't work *for you.* AA empowers many. The group requires anonymity. Being respectful of that will empower the group if AA is a route you choose. If anonymity

Having an abnormal response to alcohol is not a moral issue.

does not empower you or casts shame on your alcohol use, get it out of the dark and boldly show your sober colors. The world has options for support groups beyond AA now. Whatever you choose, a resourceful and sustainable community is available to you the second you choose it (I list a few resources in chapter 12). You get to decide to be anonymous or not.

There is no shame in having an abnormal response to alcohol. There is no shame in labeling yourself an alcoholic if it helps you make sense of your wonky relationship or lethal response to it. There is no shame in being among those whose physical bodies cannot process poison in a manner society deems dignified. There is no shame in saying no to a drink. None!

Having an abnormal response to alcohol is not a moral issue. Again, it is not your fault if you are among the millions of people unable to moderate your alcohol intake. It is not your fault if one sip leads to an obsession for more sips. It is your responsibility to recognize this truth, however. Once you do, there are loving souls happy to welcome you to the family and partner with you in a solution that works.

I'm grateful for the healthy shift today away from the stigma around abstinence. My kids, all above the legal drinking age, are free to drink or not. They don't hang out with peers who would find their lifestyle choices odd. And unlike me as a young woman, my kids don't meld to another's mold for them. They are their own potters. One of them doesn't drink alcohol. I've never asked them why, because it's a ridiculous question. They're brilliant, athletic, and emotionally intelligent. It would make more sense if I asked them why they did drink alcohol if that were the case. Society still questions saying no to a drink. A better question is, Why say yes to one?

> **Society still questions saying no to a drink. A better question is, Why say yes to one?**

Chapter 11

Dis the Dis— or Don't (It's Up to You)

You gain control by giving up control.
—Dr. Bob Rotella, sports psychologist,
author of *Putting Out of Your Mind*

As mentioned, knowing I'm an alcoholic works for me. My 12-step program works for me. The only time I got tripped up was when I came to believe it didn't, that my response to alcohol was within my control, and that I could moderate it like a distinguished gal. The more cerebral I got and the more I worked to figure out if I was "alcoholic" or not and if alcohol was a "disease" or not, the more confused I got. I was asking myself the wrong questions, because the answers to those questions don't matter. What mattered was that I was not free to live all in, and alcohol was the reason for that.

Labels are just words. They can influence how you define yourself—they cannot change how your higher power defines you. If your identity stems from who your creator says you are, then it is stainless—not stigmatic. Still, you'll want to choose words well when deciding which labels land on you and which are better peeled off and tossed to the trash.

It is vital we know what labels work for us individually and which don't and why we are choosing the lifestyle we choose. If we are not crystal clear on our purpose, then every qualified expert will influence us daily—and there are many voices on the subject and scene. In chapter 7 you got crystal clear on your own reason (your *why*) for choosing what you want, so you can stick to it regardless of what you read or hear.

I am an alcoholic, and the label is not punitive or limiting to me. What matters is what serves me. What label benefits me. I am grateful for my time spent trying on different labels. I am grateful to have landed right back where I started, an alcoholic like so many other beautiful souls on the sober journey with me.

When I look up the definition of *alcoholism* in *Merriam-Webster's Dictionary* I find "a chronic, progressive, potentially fatal condition marked by excessive and usually compulsive drinking of alcohol leading to psychological and physical dependence or addiction." Yes. That was me—when I was drinking. Once I had one sip, a compulsion for more took over. Eventually a potentially fatal psychological and physical dependence took root. The same dictionary's definition of *alcoholic* includes the synonyms *alky, juicehead, boozehound, boozer, drunk, tosspot, lush,* and *tippler.* That was me too! When I drank alcohol, I acted like those things. If I drink alcohol again, I will act like those things! None of those descriptions applies to me outside of an active addiction; however, that can change in a swallow, and knowing that is my armor of alertness. I'm not going to pretend that Tosspot Tilly is not lurking beneath the surface. That is unsafe thinking for me. Knowing the boozehound wants to be unleashed is truthful and smart. Thinking the hound does not exist because no one has heard her growl in a while is a fierce fib.

Thus, I fit the alcoholic definition, even though I've been sober for some time now. I understand why those words land stigmatically on many. They just don't land that way on me. Knowing I can turn into a lush, tosspot, or tippler with one chug from a jug motivates my sobriety and reminds me how fragile my recovery is—plus I get a kick out of the funny words.

Many of us have been labeled by a professional with various behavior, learning, or attention styles at some point. Many of these labels begin with *dis*. Some end in *ia* and some in *ism*. While they may explain some of our behaviors, do they help us arrive on the better path? Or do they separate us into a group that is destined to be less successful? For some, an *ism* is simply a word that explains a reaction to a vice. For others it is debilitating. Only you know how a word lands on you.

If a label protects you from being someone you don't want to be, use it. If a label creates a version of you that doesn't move you, others, or your environment forward, get rid of it. Dis the "dis," or don't. It's up to you. Allow labels to move you forward by using them as catapults to better things instead of excuses to continue behaviors and thoughts that don't serve you.

If calling yourself an alcoholic strengthens you and moves you into the solution and a like-minded community of healthy, energetic, sober alcoholics who build you up, then call yourself an alcoholic. If, however, the label hinders you or reminds you of an intolerable alcoholic or perhaps an alcoholic family member from whom you want to disassociate yourself, then ditch the label and the risk of associating yourself with the negativity it contains.

You get to decide what terminology will fuel you to get where you want to go. You may find that a label that works in one season no longer works in another. That's OK!

Learning to embrace grace, God's unmerited favor on me, is key to discerning helpful versus harmful labels for me. We'll discuss grace and what it means for your life in the final chapter. When I say my name is Chris, more times than not others hear *Grace*. When I order coffee from a café nowadays, I go ahead and answer *Grace* when asked for my name. It's often what they write on the cup anyway. Hearing *Grace* called out is a tangible reminder of who I am and who I am not. It's a name and label I choose to accept.

The alcoholic label was an answer that settled me. It answered the question, Why do I drink the way I do? Labeling my thing enabled me to move into the solution. I allow the labels that serve me to stick. If it doesn't serve me, I peel it off.

Choose What Sticks

Personally, I do not care for the word *disorder*. The *Diagnostic and Statistical Manual of Mental Disorders* (DSM), my bible during college and grad school, labels aspects of human nature as "disorders." It's in the title! The American Psychiatric Association publishes the manual and defines the DSM as "the handbook used by health care professionals in the United States and much of the world as the authoritative guide to the diagnosis of mental disorders. The DSM contains descriptions, symptoms and other criteria for diagnosing mental disorders. It provides a common language for clinicians to communicate about their patients and establishes consistent and reliable diagnoses that can be used in research on mental disorders."[13]

To be fair, the DSM was meant to be only one perspective. The *DSM-5* was published in 2013 and contributors include internationally recognized clinicians, scientific researchers, psychiatrists, and experts with backgrounds in psychology, social work, psychiatric nursing, pediatrics, and neurology. Participants for *DSM-5* represent sixteen countries. The latest revision also opened the process to public comments. The problem is, while the DSM is valuable and helpful, the mental health field is treating it as if it's the final word and only authority, so labels trickle down from the DSM to mental health workers to us. And there's no telling how many of the contributing experts have personally experienced the conditions they study academically.[14]

Knowledge is power, so let's use what we know about psychology to empower people, not disempower them. If a person's brain is wired to operate in an obsessive-compulsive manner, for example, that is empowering to know. That person can now use what they know to rock their world. If that person accepts that they have obsessive-compulsive *disorder*, however, it may either take the wind out of their sails or encourage them to adapt by making the label their identity

There's a difference in identifying with a label and making a label your identity.

and setting themselves apart as special (we've all met those who share their disorder within the first five minutes of an introduction). There's a difference in identifying with a label and making a label your identity. Many remarkable features make you unique, so don't limit your identity and significance to a single part of yourself.

Attention deficit disorder (ADD) and attention deficit hyperactivity disorder (ADHD) are names the mental health field prioritizes to describe people who have a set of characteristics quite common in the human population. It's helpful to identify and understand those characteristics. It would be even more helpful to empower people to thrive with and complement the way their brains work. How many people do you know with ADD or ADHD? A lot, right? Can all those folks really be the disordered ones? Again, diagnosing an individual with a "dis" sets the precedent that everyone else except them is "in order."

We get what we focus on. If we accept that we are disordered, our focus may veer toward our limitations instead of our strengths. It's up to us to decide what names are limiting or not. There's tremendous upside to having a unique brain, and each of us has a unique brain. You *are* special—just like everybody else.

Again, identifying with a label and making a label your identity are different things. The tricky part is with society slapping old and revised labels on us, like we're moving jars on a manufacturing plant's conveyor belt; we've got to be vigilant about which ones we allow to stick and which ones we peel off and toss in the trash. Some of society's stickers will peel off easily and some have been stuck on us since childhood, requiring a generous gob of Goo Gone.

How do you know which stickers you want to stick? What emotion do you love feeling? No need to answer *happy*. Remember, there's no right or wrong. Pause, get curious, and consider an emotion you love. Do that now. Do you love feeling at peace? Content? Brave? Confident? Choosing the emotional state you want for any given moment of your life is your right. You're the only person who gets to decide that. And if you're going to show up for the life you desire, you'll want to choose emotions that move you forward and ensure you're showing up—instead of staying stuck in unhelpful emotional patterns.

Feeling happy is my emotion of choice. For years, I didn't choose happiness. Instead, I believed that grinding over what I didn't love in my life would change it. I studied psychology in college and graduate school because I wanted to help others (and heal myself by analyzing my past behaviors). Grinding over those things was an honest attempt at moving forward. I proceeded the best I knew how for the season I was living at the time. However, focusing on what I wanted to leave behind only kept me stuck in it.

When I finally knew better, I shifted my focus to what I wanted, thankful that my past was the perfect environment to teach me what was necessary to become the person I am today. These days, I focus on what I'm grateful for in my present and the results I want in my future.

Move Past Your Past

We talked about getting crystal clear on what you want. Bring that outcome to mind now. Next, answer this question: Am I focusing on things that move me toward that? If so, dance party time! However, if your focus these days is more often looking back at what you want to move past, it's time to get unstuck.

I just watched the movie *The Holdovers* because I'm writing from Los Angeles, a town presently preparing for the Oscars by watching the nominated films. The line delivered to a student in a history museum by Paul Giamatti's character, Mr. Hunham, a curmudgeonly boarding school history teacher, struck me: "There's nothing new in human experience, Mr. Tully. Each generation thinks it invented debauchery or suffering or rebellion, but man's every impulse and appetite from the disgusting to the sublime is on display right here all around you. So, before you dismiss something as boring or irrelevant, remember, if you truly want to understand the present or yourself, you must begin in the past. You see, history is not simply a study of the past. It is an explanation of the present."[15] To be clear, focusing on your history is helpful—for a particular reason or season. It becomes unhelpful when you camp there. When you build your emotional home from feelings related to days gone by, you're stuck with residual pain as your primary identity.

Moving forward doesn't mean ignoring your past or pretending trauma didn't happen. It requires facing it and having the courage to ask for help from a therapist, counselor, mentor, coach, support group, or friend. Once you do that, celebrate your awareness and intention. You get to decide what you take from your past and what you don't. There's no right or wrong way to heal. And in determining the way that works best for you, continually ask yourself, *Is what I'm taking with me from this past situation moving me forward, keeping me stuck, or moving me backward?*

Knowledge about our different personality types and how to use those to interact with one another, in our business and personal lives, is powerful, like Mr. Hunham said. Some fantastic personality assessments exist to enlighten, strengthen, and encourage harmonious corporate and personal culture. Assessments such as DISC[16] or CliftonStrengths (formerly StrengthsFinder)[17] equip us to use the unique thumbprint we were born with for our benefit and the benefit of those we interact with.

The alcohol, food, and fashion industries glamorize alcohol use and being thin; then the mental health industry labels us with "alcohol use disorders" and "eating disorders" when we take it too far. How are we supposed to gauge accomplishing our social and beauty goals versus having a disorder, and who decides where the "too far" line is anyway?

A society that encourages labeling traits or behaviors as disorders places fault on the individual for coping by adapting to a disordered society.

A society that encourages labeling traits or behaviors as disorders places fault on the individual for coping by adapting to a disordered society. Take "eating disorder," for example. A person who has developed a harmful routine for eating, purging, or not eating has done that because of the skewed standards society demands (of women especially). Society's standards for beauty and body weight are disordered, not the individual. Yet "the experts" label the individual the disordered one. I've yet in my fifty-five years of life to meet one woman who has not fought, at some point, to eat (or not eat) in a manner that allows her to champion society's standard for beauty, success, and power. We are badasses doing our best and then some. Driven achievers wired for growth and success, we mold, manipulate, and maneuver ourselves to fit an unrealistic ideal because our body is the thing we can control. We cannot control society's political laws or cultural standards for our bodies, so we control what we can about our bodies. It is natural to want power for ourselves. In a culture with impossible ideals, we scrape the empowerment we can by controlling the way we eat to control the way we look. This intention is a gorgeous aspect of our human nature, which would be even more efficiently placed succeeding in other areas of enrichment. Because cultural standards are impossible, so are the goals we place on our bodies. A woman doing her darndest to keep up is not disordered; society's rules for keeping up are disordered. To label an individual disordered implies the rest of society is in order, and it's not. The mold is messed up, not the clay.

To diagnose a person with an eating disorder, who is simply striving to exist in today's world with the idealistic demands it places on them, is backward. Society's mold must be broken and reshaped to meet the individual at a human level instead of individuals continuing to strive to meet society's risky ideals.

To label an individual disordered implies the rest of society is in order, and it's not.

Alcohol use disorder (AUD) is the new term for alcoholism. Again, it places the individual at a disordered disadvantage. Alcohol is disordered. Anyone who ingests an addictive drug, such as alcohol, risks getting addicted. The drug, not the person, has the disorder. To label the individual the disordered one in a society that glamorizes, romanticizes, and idealizes alcohol is just mean. This labeling system favors the few "ordered" folks who astonishingly can drink that drug in a distinguished manner. Those of us who cannot cut the mustard are the disordered many. The mental health field creates more people with disorders than without, which does not serve people's mental health.

Like the standards we place on ourselves discussed in chapter 3, the "dis" system makes it impossibly difficult for the individual to thrive and tragically easy for them to fail.

Chapter 12

Community versus Isolation

As iron sharpens iron, so a friend sharpens a friend.
—Proverbs 27:17 NLT

WE WERE CREATED FOR COMMUNITY. ISOLATION and recovery don't mix. Facing addiction alone opens you to attack and defeat. Two are better than one, and three or more, even better!

Join a community of people who already have what you want. For example, I want relationships based on grace (nonjudgmental), listening skills, and being challenged intellectually. Connection, love, and growth are my top needs, so the communities and friends I hang around provide that. Those things are more important to me than being around people who look, talk, or dress like me. Knowing what I want and what I can do without helps me know where to place my energy.

There's no right or wrong here—you're just tapping into what works for you. So, remember what it is you want? Write it again here:

_____

_____

_____

_____

_____

Some things to consider:
- Focus on similarities, not differences. No person or group is going to be exactly like you in every area. If they were there'd be no room for growth.
- Find at least one person you can mentor and one who can be your mentor. When seeking a mentor, find someone who already has what you want and is already headed in the direction you want to go.

- Shared goals are just as or more important than shared trials. While connecting with those who've been where you've been is valuable, it may be even more valuable to connect with people who are headed where you want to go.

Exercise

Let's get even more specific about what you want in a community and mentor:

When seeking a community, how important are the following on a scale of 1 to 5 (1 being not at all important and 5 being very important)?

- Spirituality (are they of the same faith as me)—
- Intellectual Connection—
- Shared Health and Wellness Goals—
- Financial Goals—
- Shared Life Experiences—

When seeking a mentor, how important are the following on a scale of 1 to 5 (1 being not at all important and 5 being very important)?

- Spirituality—
- Intellectual Connection—
- Shared Health and Wellness Goals —
- Financial Goals—
- Shared Life Experiences—

Now that you have an idea of what you want most in connection with others, capture some ideas for where to find friendship, mentorship, and connection (note: you may find your mentor within the community you choose or outside of it):

_____

_____

_____

_____

_____

Here are some ideas to jump-start your brainstorm:
- Church groups (most community church websites list the different study or social groups you can join)
- Neighborhood recreation center groups
- Enthusiast groups (cycling, running, knitting, bird-watching, cooking, adventuring, and so forth)
- In-person and online recovery groups
- Associations
- Clubs
- The group you create

Here are some examples of online and in-person recovery communities that I like (do your own search as new groups emerge often):
- She Recovers **https://sherecovers.org/**
- The Luckiest Club **https://www.theluckiestclub.com/**
- Reframe **https://www.reframeapp.com/**
- Sober Sis **https://www.sobersis.com/**
- Alcoholics Anonymous **https://www.aa.org/**
- Celebrate Recovery **https://celebraterecovery.com/**
- A Sober Girls Guide **https://www.asobergirlsguide.com/**

Friends in my community group have a saying, "Community is the opposite of addiction." When I first heard this, I didn't grasp its meaning. *The opposite of addiction is sobriety*, I thought. I get it now, and in part two I'll share why! You'll learn what happened for me to break my sobriety, what happened to make getting it back a must for me, and why I must protect it fiercely. For me, there is no recovery without community. I know this because I exhausted my effort to recover on my own. No amount of grit, prayer, or positive thinking sustained my sobriety until I committed to community. I believe God works in my weakness—if I let Him. I believe God fuels my sobriety because I am powerless to recover on my own strength. And I believe community is the mighty tool He uses to accomplish this in my life!

PART II

———

Discovery: What Happened

Chapter 13

The Pink Cloud

The journey we take, if it is to be authentic, cannot be a private thing between ourselves and God.
—GERALD G. MAY, MD, *ADDICTION AND GRACE*

SOBRIETY HAS LAYERS. JUST AS WE EACH HAVE A different speed, method, messiness, or tidiness for packing and unpacking bags, those layers are tended to differently for everybody. For me, first there was excitement, relief, and euphoric hope. Some recovery groups call this initial euphoria the "pink cloud." I was told it would eventually fade, and the real work of showing up and feeling my feelings would begin. But my sobriety was so refreshing and life-giving that I don't remember when or if my pink cloud faded. Maybe the euphoria settled to a functional pace, probably close to the end of year one, if I had to guess. However long the so-called cloud lasted, my excitement for sobriety did not fade for over a decade, and the work of learning to sit with my feelings didn't feel like work. To me it was refreshing. My experience was such that the costs of masking my feelings for years far outweighed the cost of letting them in.

> **My experience was such that the costs of masking my feelings for years far outweighed the cost of letting them in.**

Like I said, not everybody will experience the layers in the same order I did or other people do. Recovery is not a straight line. Using any harmful soother to numb life is the opposite of living all in and showing up for the life you want. I used alcohol to numb feelings I believed would pummel me. Once I became alcohol-free, I was surprised to learn that alcohol, not feeling life, caused the real pain. Pain is natural. Numbing our pain with alcohol is not. We are naturally equipped to move forward and through pain. We are not equipped to survive the damage alcohol causes when we use it as an escape from showing up for our life.

Once alcohol was out of my way, I got to clearly see the other stumbling blocks to living a life I loved. I worked through my recovery program rigorously with my sponsor, an eighty-year-old treasure of a woman, forty-five years sober. First, I worked on my pride and stubbornness. Being intimately familiar with guilt and self-loathing, I did not understand

Pain is natural. Numbing our pain with alcohol is not.

how I could possibly work on my pride. Then one of the books we read through together described the type of pride I identified with:

> If temperamentally we are on the depressive side, we are apt to be swamped with guilt and self-loathing. We wallow in this messy bog, often getting a misshapen and painful pleasure out of it. As we morbidly pursue this melancholy activity, we may sink to such a point of despair that nothing but oblivion looks possible as a solution. Here, of course, we have lost all perspective, and therefore all genuine humility. For this is pride in reverse.[18]

That I identified with!

Since I showed up to sobriety desperate and as a last resort, I also came vulnerable and willing to be gutted. This humility is a helpful trait in any self-work and will help you go farther faster. Next, I worked on my relationships—with Scott, with our kids, with my extended family, and with my friends.

I peeled and devoured every pungent layer with fervor, immediacy, and consistency. I lived all in on creating the life I wanted. Every hour of every day was worth it, and I pinch myself daily for the life I've been able to enjoy because of recovery. I still live with fervor, immediacy, and consistency. It's how I feel most alive. My twenty-nine-year marriage is more fun, stimulating, and satisfying than ever. The closeness I share with my children is abundant and defies description with words. My relationships with friends are rich and exciting. I added a life coaching certification to my master's in counseling and started a coaching business. And I wrote (fittingly titled) *Living All In: How to Show Up for the Life You Want*. This would not have happened were I not living sober.

Second Childhood

A peculiar and magical thing happened when I first got sober at thirty-seven. I experienced a second childhood of sorts. After about ninety days, I began to think and dream about things a typical teenager might get inspired by. It was as if all the years that were taken up by overthinking and grinding over silly things and rules and all the analyzing and unwinding were just gone. Suddenly there was space in my mind and heart for new material.

It's not that I missed out on those things during my actual childhood because of drinking (I didn't have my first drink until high school). I missed out on those things initially because I lived in my head. I spent every moment of my day worrying and analyzing. I wanted desperately to remedy every feeling I had, because none of my feelings were very enjoyable.

Early in sobriety I read a lot of vampire fiction. The tween sagas were a serotonin spur for me. Then I attempted to write my own fantasy novel. Although I had fun writing it, the result was horrific. I took some creative writing courses and attended weeklong conferences. I bought myself some ice skates and began figure skating again, a sport I had competed in during junior high school. I started skiing again and taught the kids to ski at a small mountain near our hometown. I rode horses with my daughter and bikes with my sons. Sometime during that first year of sobriety it hit me that I was consistently showing up with all of me for Scott, the kids, and our pets. I did not realize how distracted I had been by my own internal chaos until I noticed and enjoyed the absence of it.

Before sobriety I was amazed at how people could just sit and watch a sporting event. Or read a book. Or sleep in. Or anything that required stillness or connection with something outside of their own thoughts. Before sobriety I was an avid runner, a terrible listener, and self-absorbed.

Sobriety first gave me a childhood, then grew me into an others-focused, genuinely concerned wife, mom, and friend. Sobriety showed me how to enjoy stillness and live and lead from my heart instead of my head. I watch sports games now. I read. I listen. I coach. And I walk and hike in addition to running.

Obsession Lifted and Dropped

I can honestly say that after about the first ninety days of sobriety, I never had a desire to drink for the next thirteen years. From 2007 to 2021 I lived free from the distraction of alcohol. I raised three children from babies to college, sober and free of threats to my presence and attention as a mom. Scott and I grew closer and stronger in our marriage. It was glorious (cue fairies dancing and birds singing).

I was told this "obsession being lifted" was a spiritual gift. There's no doubt God's hand was leading me, yet His hand was leading me even before I walked into that first meeting, and I couldn't get sober. I believe God did lead me to the meeting. Once there, though, my obsession being lifted and my ability to quit drinking were made possible because I found a community of friends to help. There's also no doubt the obsession being lifted is a scientific fact—thirty to ninety days free from your harmful habit is physiologically cleansing, thus emotionally freeing. We will expand on this in the coming chapters, to help you muster the grit necessary for your first thirty to ninety days. The pink cloud and the obsession being lifted may feel spiritual, but it is also scientific and made possible with the help of others who understand your struggle.

Usually around the one-month mark of detoxifying from the addictive ritual you used to satisfy cravings, your brain begins to recover by recalibrating its neurotransmitters like dopamine (a reward pathway) and serotonin (a mood-boosting hormone) to their natural state. This neurotransmitter reset relieves anxiety and depression and allows feelings of happiness and well-being, sometimes referred to as—you guessed it—the pink cloud.

Habitual use of your thing of choice changes your brain's responsiveness to it. While an initial hit will spike your dopamine, resulting in a pleasurable reward, over time and with tolerance, more of your thing is required to get the same amount of reward hormones released to gain the result you first experienced. Soon, any absence of your thing creates a dopamine deficit, resulting in heightened levels of stress, anxiety, or depression, nudging you once again toward taking a hit of your thing to alleviate the unwanted feelings. It's a cycle that coaxes you into believing the only solution to your pain is your thing. Really the pain is a result of chronic and habitual use of your thing, making it a vice. If you use alcohol or another thing to alleviate anxiety, stress, sleeplessness, or depression, you are clever and reasonable. Those things will be alleviated—initially. Afterward, however, your dopamine will drop below its natural level because your body has become accustomed to being spiked often, and only another hit from your vice will bring it back up. Your brain is then dependent on the vice just to feel "normal."

You deserve to have your pleasure pathways restored to a consistent level naturally. A thirty-day detox of your thing will help recalibrate your brain's feel-good chemicals so you can thrive consistently instead of sporadically.

There is much information available to you to learn about how this works and the role neurotransmitters play in addiction. Load up on the facts that lead you toward behaviors that serve you.

Not everyone who enters recovery experiences their obsession being lifted in the first ninety days like I did. Some folks white-knuckle their way through detoxing their body, and the desire to drink or use lingers for several more months. That is natural and is a beautiful case for having a firm commitment to your decision and your why.

You are durable and able to get where you want to go. If sobriety is what you want and your pink cloud didn't magically appear over your head, you still have everything you need to detox your body of alcohol. Remember that you were born sober. It is your natural state. Returning to a clean physical state is attainable. Hard, maybe. Attainable, definitely.

One magnificent thing about joining a sober community is that you'll find at least one person who has shared your same problem and questions about how to remedy that problem. Recovery is not a straight line, and there is not a packaged formula or curriculum for success. When we don't know the answer, we can lean on friends who do. Your recovery will not mimic the next person's. And when you look, you will find people who are willing to help you out of the pit, because they've been there before.

I loved the television show *The West Wing*. My favorite scene was in the Christmas episode from season 2, when Josh Lyman, the deputy White House chief of staff, is struggling with PTSD after being shot. Josh is speaking with Leo McGarry, a friend, and the White House chief of staff. Leo, a sober alcoholic in recovery, tells Josh this story:

This guy's walking down a street when he falls in a hole. The walls are so steep, he can't get out. A doctor passes by, and the guy shouts up, "Hey you, can you help me out?" The doctor writes a prescription, throws it down in the hole, and moves on. Then a priest comes along, and the guy shouts up, "Father, I'm down in this hole, can you help me out?" The priest writes out a prayer, throws it down in the hole, and moves on. Then a friend walks by. "Hey Joe, it's me, can you help me out?" And the friend jumps in the hole. Our guy says, "Are you stupid? Now we're both down here." The friend says, "Yeah, but I've been down here before, and I know the way out."[19]

Yes, rehab or doctors may help you. Yes, your higher power may help you. Your greatest outstretched hand, though, will come from the friend who's been where you're at, and sober communities are full of those friends—all over the world.

Chapter 14

Breaking Sobriety

It's our strengths rather than our weaknesses that often hold us back.

—RICHARD ROHR

WHAT HAPPENED TO TAKE ME FROM SOBER BLISS to drinking-curious? Sometimes taking the wrong road is the only way to be certain you are on the right one. By embracing sobriety and then testing if I really need to be sober, I became certain that abstinence is the only road for me. Instead of regrets, I appreciate the dead-end road I traveled because I never have to take that road again.

It wasn't until thirteen-plus years after my first sobriety date that I challenged my belief that I will always have an abnormal response to alcohol, and that it is like an allergy that can't be outgrown. Challenging this truth scrambled my belief system and required me to get a new *why* for not drinking. I was successful at thirteen years of continuous sobriety because I *believed* those things were true, and if it was true that I had an allergy then, I was going to stay away from alcohol like an allergic kid staying away from nuts. The belief system worked like magic to sustain my sobriety. Until I came to believe differently.

Belief is powerful. I watched the National Geographic documentary *Jane*. In 1960, at the age of twenty-six, Jane Goodall went into the Gombe Stream Game Reserve (today Gombe Stream National Park) in Tanzania to study chimpanzees in the wild. Selected by her then boss at the local natural history museum, Dr. Louis Leakey, Jane had no training or scientific degree. Prior to this expedition, virtually nothing was known about chimpanzees in the wild. Equipped with little more than her binoculars, notebook, and enchantment with wildlife, Jane confronted the unknown. In the documentary, present-day Jane tells the interviewer, "The only way to learn about them [animals] is when they know you're there, but they ignore you." The interviewer quips back, "Except, they could rip your face off," and Jane responds, "Well, I didn't know that. I didn't think about that! There was nobody talking about that." He asks, "There was no fear of chimpanzees in the wild?" Jane answered, "You have to realize that back then [1960], there were no people out in the field whose research I could read about."[20] Jane was not focused on danger because there was no evidence to suggest any. Her belief kept her nerves settled and her curiosity piqued. A quote from her institute's website explains her frame of mind during her time in Gombe: "A sense of calm came over me. More and more often I found myself thinking, this is where I belong. This is what I came into this world to do."[21] The narrative of a chimp ripping Jane's face off did not occur to her because there was no factual evidence from history to support it; thus, being a woman in search of truth, she believed she was safe.

Remember chapter 5: Belief = Truth + Story? Jane's truth (I'm going to Gombe to live with chimpanzees) plus her story (I'm safe) formed her belief (a calm sense that this is where I belong).

I highlight Jane's experience because it is a natural example of the wonders humans are capable of when the things we choose to believe serve us and others. It's a risky metaphor talking about my story and Jane Goodall's in the same chapter, so I hope you get my gist.

With over a decade of continuous sobriety in my toolbox, I had a rational, reasonable thought: *Perhaps I'm not an alcoholic. Perhaps the reasons I drank were to numb the discomforts and anxious feelings of my youth, which I've evolved out of now. I was the only one who thought I was alcoholic. Was there enough evidence produced to prove I am? What if I'm not? Huh ... what if I'm not?*

Implausible as it may sound, up until this point in my sobriety, I never had this thought (it never occurred to me that a chimpanzee could rip my face off). And now that my babies had left the nest, I was in a new season of life where I had more time for creating projects and thinking about what I wanted to do with the second half of my life. I had peeled so many layers that I hit a core. I was good. I was content. I was living free and all in. And I knew enough to know that it was OK to take a beat and rest in that contentment, at least for a season. I knew enough to know not to stir up chaos just for the sake of curing boredom. I knew enough to allow myself to sit still for a season and just enjoy the fruits of my self-work. Pause the growth. Marinate in the reprieve I'd been given.

So I did. And somewhere in the marinating I got curious about what it would be like to enjoy a drink. For the first time in over a decade, I wanted to be "normal" and enjoy a cocktail as effortlessly as Scott and our friends did. After all, my reasons for desiring a drink were vastly different from when I was thirty-seven. I wanted to enjoy a drink, not use it to numb life.

I love fun. I used to drink to have fun and to numb discomfort. With the discomforts I once numbed now gone, only fun remained for me at the bottom of the glass (or halfway through it), right? Nope. I was so focused on the reasons why I used to drink, I forgot the reason why I stopped drinking in 2007. Being out of touch with my why invited the once-lifted obsession to return. Again, the reasons we pick up a habit will change over time and thus are not as important as knowing our reason for setting down the habit.

I was grateful for what sobriety brought into my life, what it healed, and what it created. And at the same time, I wondered if I still needed it. I was now a fifty-two-year-old woman of sober mind. Was being of sober mind and spirit enough, or did I also need to remain a nondrinker?

Taking the First Drink

I told Scott how I was feeling and mentioned, "These are just passing thoughts though. I'll tough it out. I mean, I can't have it all, right?" Scott, in his positivity and normie growth mindset, came back with, "Why not? Why can't you have it all?" That did it. If Scott supported following through on my curiosity, I was in! (Again, know *your* why!) Together we decided I would give alcohol another go. We were headed to a birthday celebration dinner and Scott crafted a martini for me. That is what I was craving. I never really enjoyed wine or beer and was clueless to what a seltzer was since those came on the scene during my sobriety. When I started having thoughts about being able to drink again, I thought about enjoying one martini. Sucking on the green olives while sipping the vodka slowly. Letting just a hint of alcohol marinate the saltiness in my mouth. That is the taste I craved and the feeling I believed I was missing out on. That is what I believed I could invite into my life as an every now and then event and on special occasions. It went well that night. And for a few weeks following that night. It wasn't only on occasion, though. I quickly decided that I could enjoy one martini every night at 5:00 before dinner with Scott. So that's what I did.

Moderation Is Messy

The first of many moderation hiccups was, I had been so full of shame until the day I got myself to that first meeting and got sober in 2007 that the instant my sobriety date was *stained*, the shame returned, despite the fact it had no merit and I had not done anything shameful. I prided myself on my continuous sobriety, so my well-considered decision to get curious about my relationship with alcohol was now a stigma staining my *perfect record*. My rigid-thinking mind screamed "failure" for not balancing the teeter-totter.

My destructive perfectionist tendencies kicked in and the self-sabotaging thoughts returned immediately. I came to be more obsessed with the fact I broke my sober streak than I was with exploring a different relationship with alcohol, and I knew my obsession with perfection had to go if I was going to be a successful normie. That thinking had no room in a rhythmic life. If my decisions were not based on personal evolution and curiosity, I would not succeed at moderation. I needed to dump the shame, learn to drink with dignity, and carry on! After all, I'm an achiever. I do a great job at whatever I do. If I'm going to get sober, I'm going to be the best in the world at it. If I'm going to raise my tolerance and learn to moderate alcohol, I'll be the best at that too. I pushed on, determined not to give up my drinking-curious experiment as the only means to living shame-free. I thought there must be a way to shed the guilt, hang on to all I'd evolved into up to that point, *and* find out what being a mindful drinker was all about.

The tenacity of some of us doers, right?

Scott, the kids, and I love amusement parks, especially the thrill rides. There is one ride, however, that no matter how many times I've been on it (at this point I cannot count), I fall short of enjoying it. I hate it. I certainly don't lack bravery, courage, grit, gumption, or the love of a thrill. I just lack the ability to stomach that one ride. And by stomach, I mean, I cannot ride without losing my stomach, breath, and mind. I clench, claw, clasp, and close my eyes—every time. And every time starts with the mindset that *This will be a success. I've got this. All I need is within me now*, and so on. The amount of repetition, conditioning, visualization, peak performance tools, and intention I've put into riding this ride successfully (meaning enjoying it) could complete the content for a Tony Robbins conference. The attraction description is, "An accelerated (*too fast*) drop tower (*plummets at light speed*), indoor (*pitch dark*) coaster (*only goes up and down*)." The ups and downs happen randomly, so there is no indication when it will stop rocketing up or hurling down. It is a terrifying death drop of an attraction—and one that I rode again last week. I sent the photo that is waiting at the end of the ride to my kids (Scott and I have not stopped playing on our own despite the kids being flown and grown). In the photo Scott and the other seventeen passengers are laughing with hands raised, teeth showing, and posture relaxed. There are even two tiny children in the front row dabbing for the camera as if they're enjoying a spa day with good friends. Then there is me, behind the tiny dabbers, eyes shut tight, jaw clenched, shoulders hunched, and knuckles wrapped taut and white around the grab bars (which no one else seemed to know were there). Anyway, I texted the photo to the kids with the comment, "Nailed it."

The replies were, "Hahaha." "OMG this is hilarious (laugh crying emoji)!" "Such a great photo!" And my daughter, Chloé, "HAHA best thing to wake up to. At least you did it! Although—I don't know why you still do it to yourself!"

Then I replied, "That was my final time on that ride. *No mas!*"

And Chloé said, "Yeah, we shall see. Heard that before, Mama!"

I don't know if that was my last time or not. If it was, I went out swinging. If it wasn't, a park ride won't kill me. Tenacity is a strength and not everything is meant to be quit like an addiction is. The key is to know when and what to quit, and to use your tenacity in ways that serve you instead of harm you. Applying my tenacity to moderating alcohol successfully was not working; nevertheless, I rode the alcohol ride a few more times before quitting.

Tenacity is a strength and not everything is meant to be quit like an addiction is.

What I loved most about my sobriety was the freedom from the distraction and stronghold of thinking about my alcohol consumption. In my empty-nester season I had hit a point where I began to obsess about that consumption again, even though I was sober. Was my not drinking beginning to cause the same distraction as my drinking? I had to find out. In my case I had to break my perfect sober streak to grow—to know why I was abstaining and if it was still the best course of action for my life.

I had been taught that alcohol use was a progressive condition and if I returned to drinking, I would pick up where I left off and then some. That I would be worse off than the last time I drank. This belief was deeply ingrained in me, so you can imagine my fear of pushing forward in the spirit of growth and exploration—yet I can do hard things, right?

By this time the mindful drinking movement I spoke of earlier had emerged. One in which the stigma of alcoholism had been replaced by educating oneself as to the scientific effects of alcohol on the brain and body. Anonymity was no longer required. Sobriety was sexy. Non-12-step support communities emerged to offer yet a third option to drinking or not drinking—mindful moderation.

I had developed a pattern of thinking that worked if I abstained from alcohol. But what if I could moderate my drinking? What growth opportunities would moderation allow me? What if just one more ride on the death-drop would cure my fear of it, freeing me to ride whenever I wanted to? I was about to learn.

Chapter 15

The Mind Trap
of Moderation

*Remember that we deal with alcohol—cunning,
baffling, powerful! Without help it is too much
for us.... Half measures availed us nothing.*[22]
—*AA Big Book*

WE TALKED ABOUT BALANCE VERSUS RHYTHM IN chapter 3. Balance can look like needing to strike a perfect balance, which for me ignites a perfectionistic flame ready to burn everything not up to snuff down to the ground. The nutritional science majors on my college campus formed a nutrition club and wore T-shirts that read, Everything in Moderation! The term confused me then and is not my favorite now.

Some things must be in moderation, and those things will be different for all of us. For example, I love peanut butter and am able to enjoy it because it will not harm me the way it will a person allergic to it. If one day that changes, I may find a support group to help me quit peanut butter (that's how much I love it). Alcohol may not destroy the person with a peanut allergy the way it will me. For me and alcohol, moderation is messy. An even better club T-shirt for me would be, SOME Things, Not EVERY Thing (Especially Alcohol), in Moderation!

Some will say, "That's not a fair comparison, Chris. An allergic reaction is a symptom, and alcohol use is a behavior or choice." Not for me and millions of others like me. I have never been able to tolerate alcohol the way some people can. Yes, it is a choice to take the first sip or not. Once that happens, though, my brain becomes unable to make the same decisions it was able to before the first sip. I have always had an abnormal response to alcohol. So while alcohol use may be a behavior, my physical response to alcohol is a symptom.

Are you disciplined in most areas of your life? Does willpower come easily to you? Are you a driven achiever wired for growth? I am too. Except when it comes to alcohol. It does not fit into the previous list. The explanation of this lies in the fact that it is a physiological, not behavioral, issue.

There are some nonalcoholics who choose to quit alcohol for behavioral or health reasons, just as there are some non food-allergic people who choose to quit or limit a certain food for behavioral or health reasons. Knowing your *why* for limiting or omitting a substance or habit is important. One is a good idea. One is a life-or-death choice.

For many, drinking without getting drunk requires a knuckle-clenching amount of willpower and discipline. Abstaining completely is the simplest and easiest way for some because they don't have to control a substance capable of controlling them.

Balance can look like needing to strike a perfect balance, which for me ignites a perfectionistic flame ready to burn everything not up to snuff down to the ground.

I chose to add alcohol back into my life, assuming perhaps it would be as effortless to moderate for me as it is for my friends and Scott. I thought that the mature version of me could enjoy alcohol freely and socially since my older age and life lessons had eliminated all the situations that alcohol once numbed. I wasn't wrong on some occasions and very wrong on others. However the drinking occasion played out, it was not as enjoyable as I'd imagined. Also, on too many occasions it made me black out and vomit—no matter how many times I rode the ride, or how rigorous my mindful-drinking training was, the promise of safety and successful consumption was never guaranteed.

About two months into my drinking-curious experiment I realized I fiercely missed my sobriety. I longed for it back. I missed my memories, my energy, and my distraction-free lifestyle that I knew so well. I missed my authentic self. I missed sober me and the way she was able to accept God's grace, no strings attached. I missed these things more than I missed drinking. For me moderation is tedious. For me sobriety is simple.

The truth ended up being that alcohol for me is fleeting fun. No matter what glass it's in or how pretty it looks, alcohol is a drug and drugs suck. The true fun and excitement are in sobriety. Sobriety is sexy. Sobriety makes me different. Sobriety is edgy and against the grain. For me, being different is thrilling. Searching for excitement in drinking with the majority left me bored and feeling common.

Remember me being told that alcoholism is a progressive condition and if I returned to drinking, I would pick up where I left off and then some, and that I would be worse off than the last time I drank? After thoroughly testing the theory, for me it holds true. When I picked up a drink after thirteen years of not drinking, the condition had indeed progressed as I aged. I was less tolerant than years earlier. So I worked on my tolerance, believing that, with conditioning, I could become a decent drinker. The opposite was true, and the more I practiced, the less tolerant I became.

The question of whether alcoholism is a disease or not has not been answered definitively. I know it is a nasty condition. Calling it a condition, thing, allergy, or disease is not what's important to me. What I don't know is constantly evolving, so it isn't as important as what I do know. I don't know why abstinence works best for me and moderation works well for others. I do know I get what I focus on. I do know I can't drink alcohol. I'd rather focus on the benefits of an abundant life than the complexities of analyzing what doesn't work and why. Learning from my experiment how fiercely I wanted my sobriety back, I set out to get it.

Lone Tattoo

Gaining back what I once had was not as simple as I had hoped. I broke my sobriety in 2021, during the COVID quarantine and immediately after moving from my home state for the first time in my life. Not only had all my support meetings moved from in-person to online, I was also in a new state and did not know where to go for sober connection. The new friends I was meeting did not know I was alcohol-free, so there was no expectation or accountability.

Having support is key. It was easy to prioritize my recovery in my first sobriety. Once handed the solution to a major problem, you bet that solution took priority. In early sobriety, recovery was my thing. I made time for it. It was a release to a built-up pressure. Around year ten, I stopped prioritizing my recovery. Once alcohol was no longer my thing or stronghold, I came to believe I had bigger fish to fry. I attended fewer support meetings. Although I did not drink alcohol, I prioritized other areas of life from before my recovery. This went on for three more years—sober as a habit instead of a priority. Alcohol-free for routine, not survival. I took my recovery for granted. When the pandemic, a major move, and empty nesting hit—all in the same year—I did not have the vigilance or armor necessary to protect my sobriety. When it was time to embrace it a second time, not knowing yet that new groups and support systems had come on the scene since my first day one, I ventured back to a 12-step meeting in my new town.

I went one time and didn't return for a while. I spun a narrative that I had grown so far from the language they were using and the beliefs they held to. As a coach I work with others and myself daily on the language we use and narratives we tell ourselves. The word *relapse* really stung. I knew instantly upon hearing it that the word would not move me forward. It would hinder me and may even keep me stuck. *I mean, really? You all want my story to be that I screwed up and am starting over? How could I be starting over? Are we going to ignore how far I've come? All the work I've put in to gain peace, get out of my head, and become others-focused?* My personal and professional beliefs screamed *no!*

I still didn't know yet about my other support options, so I decided I would get my sobriety back on my own. I didn't need a group. To stick to my plan, I went down to my local tattoo parlor and got my new sobriety date tattooed on me. It was significant because it was my first (and to this day, only) tattoo. This would ensure I wouldn't drink again.

Here's a hilarious thing about the dark side of perfectionism: In my extreme all-or-nothing reach for the ideal,

I got this tattoo two days after my last drink! No room for error, right? Permanent ink to erase any possibility of reality kicking in. A screeching halt to the rhythm of my humanness. A perfect tattoo to end further failure. Excellent.

I knew the physiological effects of alcohol and that it would take at least ten days to leave my system, and that after ninety days, living alcohol-free would create a new pattern in my brain. I thought, *I'll be golden. Back to where I was before—living unbothered by the thought of drinking or not drinking. I could do this without a support community. Just me and my tattoo.*

So I got tattooed and went just shy of six months alcohol-free. I was back! Until I wasn't. A few days before my six-month milestone, these thoughts crossed my mind: *What if I am missing out? What if I can drink alcohol now and then? Did I give it my all? Did I really put in my best effort at drinking in moderation? Am I a quitter? I can do anything. Surely, I can drink like a person who takes it or leaves it. I just need some moderation coaching. After all, now I'm thinking about not drinking alcohol. Isn't that a stronghold? I don't want any stronghold on my life. Hate that. If I just have an occasional drink when I'm craving it, then it won't have a hold on me. I'll be free again. I'm tired of being in my head about this. I was free of this junk for thirteen years. These new thoughts must be a sign I am meant to invite social drinking back into my life. That's the only way to get out of my head about it. Yes, that's what I'll do—a drink here and there to ensure this thing doesn't hold power over me. I am powerful. I can control it, not the other way around.*

This is the thinking of a nondrinker not working her program. So—six months did erase the alcohol in my body and drinking patterns in my brain. It also erased the threat to my life that alcohol is. It erased the truth from my mind that an alcohol-free life, not a drink, is the best reward. These truths were erased because I did not have a recovery community to remind me of these things.

Instead, I motivated myself by listening to sober podcasts and joining a couple of online groups that met over Zoom calls for support. At first this was refreshing motivation to remain alcohol-free; however, it was not a sustainable way for me to recover. What I learned later was I needed the in-person camaraderie of a like-minded community.

An alcohol-free life, not a drink, is the best reward.

It was as if the more knowledge I gained on my own, from behind a screen, the more capable I believed I'd be at moderating my alcohol intake. So I picked up a drink again and I realized the opposite was true. Not right away—not even the first week. It was maybe a few weeks in before I realized I needed to stop drinking again for good—and I could not do it alone. I needed real friendships and people who would notice if I was absent.

My kind tattoo artist fixed my first and only tattoo to something even more special to me, and I moved forward in search of a fresh community.

Chapter 16

Recovering Sobriety

Addiction is an adaptation. It's not you—it's the cage you live in.
—Johann Hari

WHAT I LEARNED WAS THAT WHILE I HAD evolved, matured, and changed, alcohol had not. It was just as perilous and sneaky and threatening to my emotional and physical states as it had been thirteen years earlier. I must be vigilant. I don't live according to many rules. In this area, however, rules were necessary for continued freedom from the distraction of alcohol.

A stronghold on your life is when something you are thinking about has become an obsession, thus a distraction to living the life you want. My decision to pick up a drink after years of continuous sobriety was not spontaneous. I discussed it with Scott and prayed over it before making the decision.

The point of discussions, prayers, and thoughtful meditation kept coming back to one question: If, after being free from any desire to drink alcohol for over a decade, that desire had returned and begun to invade my thoughts, is that a stronghold? My once-lifted obsession returned and consumed my thoughts again, so my answer was yes, not drinking had become as much of a stronghold for me as drinking once was. And no matter how many tools I used to ride out the craving, the curiosity about breaking my stint of sobriety to see what kind of a drinker my matured self was continued to linger in my mind. My quest for dignified moderation delivered blow after blow, and with each one I climbed back to my feet for another jab—until the night I stayed down.

The night of my last drink I drank in what appeared to be a normal manner—on a golf cart at a Fourth of July golf tournament with Scott and good friends. Classy enough. I kept pace with my girlfriend's drinks thinking this was safe, since she is not a heavy drinker and I've never seen her drunk. My plan to drink like the normies around me collapsed by the time Scott brought me home sick and in a blackout. I don't know what happened in the final hours of the evening. I know that alcoholism progressed in me over time, and like the warning to my young son with a nut allergy, on this night it almost killed me.

Many in recovery don't know exactly why the thing that got them sober was the thing that got them sober. I've heard in recovery rooms that rock bottom is not something you hit; it is something you feel. For me it was not the severity of the bottom but the decision to quit digging. The choice to get off the death-drop ride and commit, with supportive accountability, not to ride it again. The choice to change my language from "Quitters don't quit" to "Winners quit to survive."

> **For me it was not the severity of the bottom but the decision to quit digging.**

Two mornings after my last drink (because the morning after I couldn't move) I instinctively went screeching back to my local 12-step clubhouse. Unlike the first time I checked it out in my new town, this time I was home. The difference was, in addition to being down for the count, unable to face another jab, I was also not focused on differences, or the lexicon, or all the reasons I shouldn't be there and why it wouldn't work. I was done with rationalizing, romanticizing, and trying to be something I am not. Ringing the bell on my fight with alcohol allowed me to show up in a support community solely focused on why it would work, why I wanted to be there, and on similarities I had with the people in the room. I was with family.

Currently, I live free again of the stronghold of drinking as well as the stronghold of not drinking. How? In the next section I will share what works for me and how my story can help you.

Exercise

Lock in what you've learned so far by getting clear on some key things about you.

Ask yourself:

Is it possible that I entertained an obsession or the habit I now want to get rid of, not out of weakness but out of strength? _____

_____

_____

Did I use that habit to survive? To cope? _____

_____

_____

Did it serve me in some way for a while? If so, how?

_____

_____

Is it serving me now? _____

_____

_____

Will it serve me moving forward? _____

_____

What other strengths do I have that would serve me better? _____

_____

_____

What are some healthy obsessions and coping habits I could pick up? _____

_____

_____

What do I know now, because of the road that I traveled, that I didn't know before? _____

_____

_____

Chapter 17

Tipsy-Free Tips

Failure doesn't mean you're worthless—
it means you must look for another route
to achieving your worthwhile goals.
—Jay Shetty

Sharing Is Self-Caring

ONE COMMON THREAD AMONG SOBRIETY SUPPORT groups is sharing stories. It's what binds groups together. While not all stories will resemble yours, all stories are valuable. Sharing your story—whether it's in a journal only you will see or aloud to a trusted person or group of people—will make your experience even more real and safe. Kept to yourself, you'll risk romanticizing your story and setting yourself apart as special or significant. Remember pride in reverse? Recovery requires humility, and humility does not wallow in self-focused misery. It gets vulnerable and shares bravely. When your experience becomes significant and egocentric, it becomes untouchable, thus unhealable. Unrecoverable. Again, you and your story are special—just like everybody else!

> When your experience becomes significant and egocentric, it becomes untouchable, thus unhealable. Unrecoverable. Again, you and your story are special—just like everybody else!

Humility and vulnerability allow me to share my story and words with you. I want to celebrate where I am now as well as what got me here. I want to remember that sobriety is a gift, not a chore. A lifestyle, not an event. I want to honor my past, present, and future. Of course, sharing is not easy for me. It's embarrassing and pricks at my pride. That's why I must do it.

I'm inspired by the theme of accepting help. My first day one lasted from when my kids were babies until they left the nest, when I thought I was "good" and deserved a drink. The suckiness of inviting alcohol back into my life for a season taught me that I didn't deserve a drink; I deserved to thrive in my sober lifestyle. Drinking wasn't a reward, my sobriety was. I read books and approached a new sobriety intellectually and on my own, until I asked for help and joined a new support community. What's working for me now is that I got over myself and accepted help. I realized

> **The illusion of control leaves no room for appreciation of people and things just as they are— flawed and fabulous.**

I'm not ahead of anyone else. We are all part of the same family of souls. We all have ups and downs, and if I ask, there is always help in sober communities, no matter the group. Sobriety is ambitious and attainable when done in community.

Oh-Well Effect

Rigid thinkers tend to go to extremes. If it's not perfect, it's trash. If I had one drink I may as well have four. Or ten. If I'm starting over on day one, oh well, I'll start tomorrow (and go balls to the wall today).

The furthest extreme I can think of a perfectionist going is also the most tragic, which is, "Life must be a certain way or not at all." This way of living spits in the face of grace. Unmet expectations become failures, and the inability to control that which lies outside our control consumes us. The illusion of control leaves no room for appreciation of people and things just as they are—flawed and fabulous.

I got sick of having more than one day one. I got sick of oh-welling it. I like to keep track of my sober days now that I have strung together significant time. It fuels me to celebrate. Before I strung together several days in a row, however, the counting deflated me. Pay attention to what works best for you to recover. Do what energizes you and do away with what exhausts you. There are no recovery police ensuring you restart your counter every time you have a slipup. Keeping count of sober days or not is your choice. Again, do what works best for your recovery. To know what that is, run your lifestyle choices through this filter:

- Does it keep me more focused on what is working than on what isn't working?
- Does it energize me to focus on what I have or cause me to focus on what's missing?
- Does it encourage a helpful belief that life is happening for me or an unhelpful belief that life is happening to me?

If you're focused on the negatives, your energy will move toward those negatives. You deserve to focus on the sober lifestyle you want instead.

Sobriety Is Not a Competition

You can't win sobriety. I love to run and occasionally will enter a *fun* run. I emphasize fun because I have yet to make a competitive run *fun*. Recently I ran in our neighborhood's Independence Day run. Telling myself I would keep the competition friendly and low-key, I sprinted off the starting line and continued to overexert myself beyond my level of training until I crossed the finish line.

Throughout the race I was certain I would place first in my age group. Surely, they had a fifty and up category. Once finished, I nearly collapsed and barely thwarted throwing up. Proud I did neither, I gathered gusto to ask the person recording finishing times when the results would be posted and how we would know our placement since they did not ask for my age at registration. "We just gave a medal to the top three women over fifteen years old," he said. "Way to go getting a participation medal."

If you're focused on the negatives, your energy will move toward those negatives. You deserve to focus on the sober lifestyle you want instead.

What!? Fifteen and up? I was competing against fifteen-year-olds? It was rigged. What a setup! I was miffed. I spent the entire rest of the day with chills and a nasty cough from pushing myself physically to get my medal. So much for being first in my age group for the neighborhood *fun* run.

This is what reentering sobriety was like for me. I was so focused on winning sobriety, coming in first, and being recognized and rewarded for my previous years of abstinence that I didn't pay attention to the fun and rewards sobriety offers. I was more focused on the fact that I had stained my record than I was on the beauty of reclaiming my healthy mind and physiology.

I wanted to shout from the rooftops, "I won! I've strung together thirteen years more than the next guy of no sips of alcohol!" The problem with this thinking is . . . what happens once I take a sip? Guilt, shame, and a pitiful esteem plummet.

Resentments

A note about resentments and not harboring them. How do you move on from resentments? By knowing that you cannot change others. You can, however, change how their behavior lands on you. Write that down. Recite it over and over. Condition it into your nervous system. Other people have a right to be themselves and you have a right to feel the emotions you want to feel. Once a person shows you who they are, stop expecting them to be somebody else. To expect others to be different is not fair to you or them. If you didn't get the parents, in-laws, or coworkers you expected, you are unique—just like the rest of us. What did you get? What are you grateful for? Write those things down. Focus on what shimmers, not life's dimmers. Whatever you focus on, there you will go.

You cannot change others. You can, however, change how their behavior lands on you.

If you allow it to, being disappointed in your lot can be fiery fuel to place your energy on serving others, the community you were allotted, and your space on this earth. You get one magical, wild lifetime. Do you want to use up hours wallowing in resentments or pondering your unmet expectations? What do you want to use it for?

No Fair!

Some of us rigid thinkers have a heightened sense of what we believe is right or wrong and thus fall into the trap of holding others and ourselves accountable to an impossible standard. We tend to see the world as what's fair and what's not instead of accepting that nothing is fair, even, or perfect in our world, this side of eternity. We are not born with a manufacturer's guarantee our lives

Once a person shows you who they are, stop expecting them to be somebody else.

will be addiction-free. The downside of thinking things should be fair is it creates self-pity or harmful emotions when disillusioned standards aren't met. Since the world is not balanced even Stephen, that disillusionment finds its home in emotions such as anger, depression, or anxiousness, which can each become an emotional home comfortable to us if we're unaware.

If we consistently give our circumstances or other people the power over our emotions, we will stay frustrated. If we accept what we can control—ourselves—we will find peace and acceptance of the way the world is and the behavior of others in it. Consistently ask yourself, *What can I control in this situation?* The answer will be you, your emotions, your mindset, and your actions. You cannot control other people. You cannot control the physiology you were born with. Once you allow others the right to make their own choices and allow yourself the right to sit contently in yours, you'll find peace.

Abundance Mindset

Difficult life changes and being different build character. Reframe disappointments as what's gained instead of lost. Choose words and actions that do that. Then notice what happens inside your soul. An abundance mindset speaks of what's gained. A scarcity mindset speaks of what's lost.

Give this a whirl: For a week, speak only about what's gained—and see what happens. *What if instead of losing weight, you gain lightness? Instead of quitting an addiction, you gain clarity (i.e., gain sobriety instead of quitting drinking)? What if you stop being a victim and start being a victor? What if you grieve by honoring the beauty that person or thing added to your life?* You get what you speak. It becomes your truth. Choose your words wisely.

Exercise

The sober life you desire is a lifestyle, not an event. You must envision yourself in that lifestyle and then focus on moving toward it. Here is an exercise to get crystal clear on the person you want to grow into. Thoughtfully consider the following questions:

- What do I want and who do I want to become? Picture this person and then ask:
- What am I wearing?
- What am I hearing, seeing, smelling, and feeling?
- Who am I hanging out with?
- What is my spiritual life like? (Where, how, and with whom do I worship? What is my prayer life like?)
- What are my daily activities (from waking to sleeping)?
- What is my typical week like?

Now, being as detailed as possible, describe your future:

- Social life
- Alone time
- Thought life
- Work life (workspace, associates, and so forth)
- Living space
- Physical wellness
- Technology and digital habits

Now, using your answers to these questions, write a letter from your future self. Get into character. Envision the person you'll become. Step into that identity. See it, feel it. Act as if you are already yourself from the future you want. Now write what you want to say to your present self in a letter. This is not a letter to mail yourself later. Use it now. Read, recite, or watch a video of you reciting the letter when you wake up and before you go to bed. Do what works best for you to condition your future vision.

Recap

Let's round out what we've learned so far with a few more tipsy-free tips, before moving on to part 3:

- Discover what need or desire you quench with alcohol. Then brainstorm alternative methods to address that. Create new, rewarding rituals from your answers.
- Research the effects of alcohol on your physical and mental health, productivity, relationships, and emotions. You'll discover that alcohol intensifies anxiety, depression, memory loss, bad skin, poor sleep, dehydration, and more.
- Recognize the marketing messages bombarding you. Although the tide is changing, plenty of cultural norms still bank on you accepting alcohol as the ideal way to connect, celebrate, or take the edge off after work. For every romanticized benefit of alcohol, there are more downsides.
- Choose a mocktail and skip the drawbacks. There's an ever-expanding world of exciting, alcohol-free options on menus, online, and in stores.
- Embrace a mindset of abundance rather than scarcity. When you perceive something as gained, that mindset points you in the direction you want to

go rather than lingering on lack. For example, if
sobriety is the best path for you, speak and think of
gaining sobriety instead of quitting drinking.

- Consciously consider your commitment to abstinence ahead of time and stick to it. Hunger, mood,
blood sugar, energy level, and peer pressure often
dictate in-the-moment decisions.

PART III

Recovery: What It's like Now

Chapter 18

Heed the Greed

It will be the thing that ends us.
Greed will be the thing that kills us all.[23]
—HELEN MIRREN AS CARA DUTTON

ELEN MIRREN'S CHARACTER, CARA DUTTON, from the hit show *1923*, ponders the greed of society in the year 1923 this way: "I wonder what that says about us as a species. I mean, it's not as if women were running a straight razor down their legs a decade ago. They invented a razor specifically for women when no need for one existed, and then invented the need."[24]

It's silly we have entire books about *not* drinking. That's the world we live in, though, a drinking world. We also live in a world obsessed with unrealistic body size that markets wellness and diet products to us, then expects us not to get tripped up with food issues and addictions. There is hilarious sobriety content on social media (Instagram hosts a vast sober community) that keep me laughing about the absurdity of the situation. Laughing with others who share your same goals is a magnificent way to stay motivated. One of my favorite stand-up bits is by comedian Jim Gaffigan:

> When you don't drink, people always need to know why too. They're like, "You don't drink? Why?" This never happens with anything else. "You don't use mayonnaise? Why? Are you addicted to mayonnaise? Is it OK if I use mayonnaise? I could go outside..."[25]

Society today is motivated by the same and different greed that existed in 1923. We live in a culture that pushes to invent a need where no need exists. We were all born sober. It is our most natural state. None of us thought we needed alcohol or diet products until the world sold us the idea that we did.

The audacity of selling vices to the public was never more obvious to me than when I was fighting to recover my sobriety in 2021. During my first sobriety I was not bothered by marketing, perhaps because of the consuming amount of brain power and time spent raising babies at home. I was out of touch and tune with media and limit-less digital entertainment (ours consisted of commercial-free Netflix DVDs that came in the mail). Also, I had the safety of my sober group. The second time, because I sought sobriety on my own, media images romanticizing alcohol seemed to bombard me when I least expected it. The lack of accountability within a community lowered my guard. An image would trigger a craving and with only myself (and my tattoo) to fight it, I'd lose on too many occasions.

One of my favorite things I am privileged to do is snow ski. Relocating to a different state was fun because we moved within driving distance of Colorado's ski hills. One ski day with Scott and our son Nick, I unexpectedly got rattled by a beer ad in a bathroom stall. A sunny day enjoying fresh powder, I was focused on family, health, fresh air, and fun. The thought of adding alcohol to the day didn't cross my mind because my skiing memories had been made as a child (sober) and during my sober years. I didn't realize it initially, however, that day was my first time skiing since I'd broken my sobriety and was working to gain it back. This fact is important because of schemas—in psychology, a cognitive framework or concept that helps organize and interpret information. We will jump back to schemas in a second.

I stopped at the lodge to use the bathroom, walked through the bustling bar area, warm with a fireplace, laughter, and liquor, and had a new thought—having a drink at that bar would be cool. I promptly told myself, *No harm, it's just a thought*, and continued ski boot stomping my way to the restroom stall. In a safe space at last, I began the process of unpeeling puffy layer after puffy layer, which takes for-ev-er when you really must go. Finally seated, I was faced with a beer poster on the back of the stall door advertising the local brew, newly available on tap exclusively at the bar I still needed to exit through. The poster was aesthetically inviting, and the tempting thoughts returned immediately. I was fuming. Here I was, minding my beeswax, shielded from the outside world, yet the world was there too, in my safe space. The dirty marketing rascals know we will be in the bathroom stall awhile (because of the puffy layers) and that we must walk through the bar to exit.

This ignited my awareness that this ruse didn't just want to sell beer. It is intended to keep me and others like me stuck in a cycle of using and buying the things we've habitualized. That awareness fueled me to exit through the bar with a suck-it grin and enjoy the rest of the ski day with Scott and Nick. Being subliminally pitched what I should want made me vehemently not want it by the end of my bathroom break. Sadly, this push is motivated by power and economic gain. Although this push is growing in muscle, so is our cultural awareness of these subliminal plants.

Now back to schemas. Simply put, a schema (plural: schemas or schemata) is a pattern of behavior and thinking we use to interpret the world. It is a generalization of past experiences that forms a pattern of thought. Our brain uses schemas as a shortcut to interpret vast amounts of information absorbed daily about ourselves and our environment. It is a fancy word for pattern. Our brain assumes a thing is a certain way because it was that way in the past. For example, I was thrown by the temptation that hit me when I walked through the bar because, in my memories of skiing with Scott and the kids (which were all made in sobriety), I had not associated alcohol with a family ski day before, thus I had not formed a schema that supported the temptation.

There are unconscious behaviors in all humans that marketers have learned to leverage for their benefit.

The reason this is important to know is so you can be vigilant about the schemas that have formed in your brain since childhood. There are unconscious behaviors in all humans that marketers have learned to leverage for their benefit. You are smarter than the greedy parts of society. Your past experiences do not have to interpret your present and future experiences, yet if you are not vigilant, they may subconsciously. Stay sharp. A pattern is not a pattern unless you say so. Awareness, then curiosity, are your tools for creating patterns that serve you and dumping those that don't.

Liar, Liar, You're on Fire

Then we will no longer be immature like children.
We won't be tossed and blown about by every wind
of new teaching. We will not be influenced when
people try to trick us with lies so clever they sound like
the truth. Instead, we will speak the truth in love.
—EPHESIANS 4:14–15 NLT

Alcohol is a sneaky liar to me, and so is your harmful habit to you. If you're looking for a reason to live free, here it is: Your vice does nothing for you. To believe it does is to believe a lie. The temporary high or relief is overshadowed a thousand times by the consistent feeling of well-being you'll have from living free of it. So why do we believe the lie? Because we believe we are giving up something precious. You can stop believing that one now. We live in a world that sells lies. A world that wants us to believe we are missing out if we don't partake in the very things that can hurt us (alcohol, sugar, wellness enhancers, diet products, gambling, gaming, and sexualized media images). It's not true. The opposite is true. You will find the abundant joy you are looking for only when you are free of the harmful things you believe will bring that fun and freedom. Sure, the first thirty to ninety days may suck. That's when to find your grit and muscle through. On the other side of ninety days lies your freedom. The lie is that you won't make it to the other side. But you are smarter than that lie.

If you've never tasted alcohol and wonder why in the world someone's curiosity wants to give this poisonous substance that does nothing for them a go, it's because we live in a world that works hard to sell us on the idea that it will improve our life. Don't buy the lie. Be aware of what you want and who or what is selling you on an idea leading you in an opposite direction of what you want. It comes from our parents, friends, family, country songs, marketing, and every restaurant you've ever walked into.

Buddy the Elf, from the beloved holiday movie *Elf*, had only experienced the real Santa Claus and the real North Pole before traveling to New York City, so he knew how to spot a fake when he delivered the line to a shopping mall Santa, "You sit on a throne of lies!" Unless you have been living in the North Pole, you know that this world wants to sell you a pile of lies.

> If you're looking for a reason to live free, here it is: Your vice does nothing for you. To believe it does is to believe a lie.

Maybe alcohol's future will be like that of tobacco and other trends past generations once believed were harmless. I grew up doing things my kids' generation cautiously avoids, such as not wearing helmets and seat belts, riding on the gas tank of my dad's motorcycle, walking to school alone, and drinking from the garden hose.

I read an anonymous quote online: "Sobriety is not a health trend; it is a terrifying, enlightening and rebellious act in a world that puts drinking on a pedestal."

This resonates with me. I must keep in mind that while there is a vast amount of scientific evidence that alcohol has zero benefits and only causes harm to the human body, I still live, for now, in a culture that uses it like water. It is everywhere. Until that changes, I must be in a sober community; otherwise, I am the fish swimming upstream in a raging river of ethanol.

Sobriety today is ambitious. It's rebellious. I didn't need the health trend to change before choosing to eat healthy. I didn't need the seat belt law to be put in place before wearing my seat belt—all it took was one weird eighties driver's ed film in high school to convince me of that. Sobriety, however, is different. Even though I am convinced in my gut I don't want alcohol because it is bad for me as a human, the decision to abstain in today's culture is a bigger ask and comes with pushback by lovely, well-meaning people. Today, your and my decision to live alcohol-free takes effort, vigilance, and maintenance. And we've got this! Way to go, getting to this point in the book. Let's keep going. You are on fire!

Chapter 19

What Do You Want?

We had to drink because times were hard or times were good. We had to drink because at home we were smothered with love or got none at all. We had to drink because at work we were great successes or dismal failures. We had to drink because our nation had won a war or lost a peace.[26]
—*Twelve Steps and Twelve Traditions, Step Four*

WHY I DRANK DOES NOT MATTER AS MUCH AS why I don't. I used to tirelessly come up with answers to why I drank. I thought if I knew why I was using alcohol and what I was soothing with it, I could cure my obsession with it and become a normie. There was never one answer though. I drank to cure boredom. I drank to feel. I drank to not feel. I drank to quiet my mind. I drank to entertain my mind. I drank to feel calm. I drank to feel wild. I drank to feel brave. I drank to feel fear. I drank to remember. I drank to forget.

Even if I had sleuthed the answer to why I drank, the answer would have changed over time. Finding a soothing solution works temporarily to satisfy your reason for picking it up. Eventually the soother becomes a ritual, then an addiction, then when the reason for the habit fades, the addiction remains.

> **Finding new reasons for continuing an addiction won't serve you. Finding new reasons for breaking free from that addiction will.**

For example, a person may have picked up a behavior in college because it fit the culture of the moment. The reason they picked up a habit was for fun and social connection. If the thing becomes an addiction, then the person continuing to party like a college student after graduation is no longer doing it for college social connection; they are continuing because they are addicted—even though they may attempt to find new explanations for why they continue the behavior.

Finding new reasons for continuing an addiction won't serve you. Finding new reasons for breaking free from that addiction will. The bottom line for me is, the various feelings I sought to gain with alcohol were fleeting and cheap imitations of the authentic aliveness I feel now in sobriety. The reasons I choose sobriety matter far more than the reasons I drank.

Why you do what you no longer want to do is not as important as *why* you want to be free of that behavior. What do you want instead and why do you want it?

What do you want?

_____

Why do you want it?

_____

What will it cost if you don't get it?

_____

What will you gain if you do?

_____

Exercise

Here comes one of the life-coachiest assignments you'll get from me: Create a vision board to prioritize the things you want for you over the things others want for you. I want to energize you, not blow your mind with confusing concepts. The best athletic coaches in the world focus on fundamentals. Likewise, while evolving, testing, and incorporating new concepts that work, I cherish foundational tools that have been tried and proved true over time—and the vision board is a keeper.

Prioritize the things you want for you over the things others want for you.

So here we go: You can make two boards or one board with a line down the middle. The key is to build a positive and a negative vision board for what is battling for your attention versus what you want instead.

Title the positive board: Invigorating Messages That Support My Goals

Title the negative board: Messages Constantly Battling for My Attention

Get creative and use words, media images, and messages that influence you for both boards. Be thoughtful and thorough and leave room to add new content as you notice it moving through your environment each day. Be aware and stay curious!

Chapter 20

Choose Your Hard

*At some point, everything's gonna go south on you...
everything's going to go south and you're going to say,
"This is it. This is how I end." Now, you can either
accept that, or you can get to work. That's all it is. You
just begin. You do the math. You solve one problem...
and you solve the next one... and then the next. And
if you solve enough problems, you get to come home.*
—MARK WATNEY, *THE MARTIAN*

NOW THAT YOU KNOW WHAT YOU WANT AND what's distracting you from living the life you want, it's time to get after it. Let's get gritty. Embracing sobriety is badassery at its finest. You're a revolutionary because you do hard things. Most of us reading this are part of today's comfortable culture, no longer fighting wild animals and elements for survival and every meal. With a luxury coffee shop on every corner, not getting our custom drink fix is a modern danger for some. Just because the society you live in does things a certain way, that does not mean you have to. You are a stellar human who already has everything you need to break generational and cultural patterns. You get to establish the habits that work for you!

As I mentioned, I was not long into my drinking-curious experiment when I knew I fiercely wanted my sobriety back. The problem was, even though my heart wanted to go back, my brain was addicted. The obsession was not getting lifted even though I wanted it to. And without a community to support me through craving society's comforts, I continued to give in to them. I needed fellow rebel advocates to fight cultural norms with me. On my own, my body stayed weak even though my spirit was strong. I relate to the apostle Paul, who wrote in Romans 7:19, "I want to do what is good, but I don't. I don't want to do what is wrong, but I do it anyway" (NLT).

I'd go a while alcohol-free and then something would trigger a craving, and that trigger could be anything from a social event to a song to a thought. Triggers will come for you in your finest moments, your lowest moments, and when you least expect them. If you do not know what you want and have not committed to getting that result no matter what, the rationalizing will take over. In my case, caving to a craving ignited the oh-well effect, and I was on a roll until hitting the next pain point motivating me to quit again. The cycle was exhausting.

Getting sober again was hard—staying stuck in the exhausting cycle was way harder. I needed to get leverage on myself to choose my hard, and I'll help you get leverage on yourself with the exercise in chapter 21. The truth is, your cravings didn't start in an instant, and they won't end in one either. That's where the grit comes in.

The great thing about your habit is, it's just one thing. A strong little hellion, yes. But you are stronger. Once you decide you want it out of your life and make sobriety a must, it will help

> **The truth is, your cravings didn't start in an instant, and they won't end in one either. That's where the grit comes in.**

to see the little miscreant in its true light: a sneaky liar, yet just one thing. Here's the truth: *Abstinence is parting with one thing to gain everything. Addiction is clinging to one thing even though it means losing everything.*[27] So how do you want to play this thing? Are you a warrior who gets gritty and abstains from one thing to gain everything, or will you risk everything by staying content in your culture of comfort, in a false attempt to have it all?

Alex Honnold is one of this generation's greatest adventure athletes and rock climbers. Jimmy Chin is a world-class professional mountain athlete, *National Geographic* photographer, and Academy Award–winning film director who made the documentary *Free Solo*, which follows Honnold up the first-ever free solo ascent of El Capitan in Yosemite National Park. "Free solo" means without ropes and alone! And Alex climbed the 2,900 feet in three hours and fifty-six minutes. With. No. Ropes! Alex Honnold is a fear expert. I heard him answer Chin in an interview, "The correct way to manage fear, I think, is to gradually broaden your comfort zone, until your comfort zone includes things that previously seemed impossible."[28]

Do you fear quitting your thing is impossible for you? It isn't. Outside of your comfort zone, yes. Impossible, no. To broaden your comfort zone successfully, broaden it gradually. This is what one day at a time is about. You're not abstaining from your thing forever. You're abstaining for today. When tomorrow comes, you'll repeat this pattern. If an entire day is an unwieldy chunk, abstain for one hour, five minutes, or just for this moment.

Do you fear quitting your thing is impossible for you? It isn't. Outside of your comfort zone, yes. Impossible, no.

Are you doing the thing you want to quit right this second? If not, you can break free of it because you're already doing it! You just put the first bead on a string of success and are ready for the next one. Recovery is a process of stringing together moment after sober moment. Soon you'll have strung together a chain of moments, each valuable link another layer of yourself uncovered.

Here's a trick I use on myself and my kids when feeling overwhelmed or fearful about anything. I say: *Show me in this room* [or wherever they are] *where the problem is.* The answer is most likely—*it's not in this room.* Then I point out that if the problem is not in the room or immediate physical location, it's in our head or somewhere outside what we have control over in the present moment. Be where your feet are. Manage what is in your control to manage in the present moment.

Honnold does not speak of getting rid of fear. He gives us insight into managing it. New adventures are scary and fearing them is natural. Again, your cravings didn't start in an instant, and they won't end in one either. Sure, moving forward is scary, and staying stuck is even scarier.

Quitting an addiction is hard—a life of addiction is harder. Getting in shape is hard—an unhealthy lifestyle is harder. Working for a boss you believe is difficult is hard—unemployment is harder. Studying is hard—not completing your degree is harder. Not popping off to the police officer you believe didn't have a right to question you is hard—communicating with fellow inmates is harder. Menial, repetitive tasks like laundry and housework can be hard—not having loved ones to clothe and clean for is harder. Write down your own examples of what's hard about doing an uncomfortable thing versus what's even harder about not doing it.

Ask yourself: *What is the cost of quitting my habit? What is the cost of not quitting my habit?*

There is no even Stephen. There is no consistent state of ease. The life you love with the people you love is worth doing hard things for. We love to feel good, and sometimes this is confused with not doing hard things. No matter how accessible and instantaneous the world tells you gratification is, sustainable satisfaction is still the result of effort.

Author's Note: I understand that even in the US today there is poverty, and in marginalized communities, taking even one step to better one's life might seem impossible. I understand access to free recovery groups is still impossible for some, either because of lack of transportation, physical ability, or incarceration. I acknowledge it does take some amount of privilege to make the choices to better one's life and overcome addiction. Part of my personal sober lifestyle involves contribution and being of service by bringing the message of recovery to prisons, hospitals, and institutions.

Chapter 21

That First-Hit Feeling

*I only write when I am inspired. Fortunately,
I am inspired at nine o'clock every morning.*
—ATTRIBUTED TO WILLIAM FAULKNER

HUMANS LOVE TO FEEL GOOD. I AM ADDICTED TO feeling good. Achievers accomplish feeling good by working out, eating clean, taking our vitamins, setting goals, achieving goals—and spiking our serotonin and dopamine with things that may become addictive. A hit of our thing rewards our pleasure pathways and makes us feel good—for twenty minutes or so. It's these minutes we crave and obsess over. Once that craving is lifted by taking the first hit, the obsession for more flares up to get that first-hit feeling back—to no avail.

With time and habituation, the feel-good chemicals in our brain begin to get rewarded before the actual hit, just at the thought and anticipation of the hit. With repetition and conditioning, our brains learn to crave the excitement of the first hit.

For many, the awareness that this is the case is enough to not start a harmful cycle in the first place—not take the first hit. For others, perhaps deeper into the addictive cycle, we need tools to grit our way out of the addiction trap and sustain our feel-good comfort zone.

Ah, the euphoria of that first hit from our thing! It excites, relaxes, calms, and energizes, all in a matter of seconds. There's no denying this. There's also no denying that afterward, we spend who knows how long attempting to recover that initial feeling. We will never attain it, and bless us, we are go-getters, so we give it our all. We attempt the death-drop ride over and over again in hopes that the next time will be the successful one. The saying we learned in chapter 6 holds true: "The definition of insanity is doing the same thing over and over again and expecting a different result." We strategize and live in our heads making up heinous reasons, scenarios, and excuses for why and how to extend or recover that feeling. This is how benders are born.

Do you find yourself spending the rest of the day or night trying to maintain that first feeling buzz? Or spending the entire next day nursing a headache, chaotic blood sugar levels, or remorse? Oh, the physical and emotional toll addiction takes on us—from rationalizing why we deserve that first-hit feeling to beating ourselves up for not being able to enjoy, moderate, or maintain it.

Stop the insanity. You didn't do anything wrong. These are the manipulative effects of the thing you're addicted to (that sneaky liar). You are not flawed. Your habit of choice is!

Exercise

Here are some questions to use when a craving hits. Getting curious and real about your answers will prompt you to visualize the effects of taking that first hit on fast-forward as you consider if that twenty minutes or so is worth it.

1. What exactly am I craving? What physical, mental, or emotional feeling am I searching to quench?

2. How will the initial consumption of my thing of choice quench that feeling? Be specific. Bullet point each benefit you'll initially experience.

3. Go through each bulleted benefit and write down how long that feeling will last when you quench it with your habit.

4. Write down how long you will spend attempting to recover that feeling once it wears off in that many minutes or hours.

5. Go through each bulleted benefit and brainstorm at least one other way you could get that feeling without your habit. For example: *One sip of alcohol relaxes my digestion. So does walking, stretching, meditation, a warm blanket or bath, and so forth.*

6. Write down how long your beneficial feeling will last when obtained via a healthier means.

7. Which is more exciting for you? Which is more sustainable?

8. Would you rather have a longer-lasting excitement/ high or the twenty-minute version?

9. You're doing great. Let's keep going.

10. If your answer is, *I'll take the twenty-minute version, Chris. Duh. Nothing can replace that,* great honesty! Let's unpack the future of this decision further.

11. Take your answer from question 4 (how long will you spend trying to recover that feeling once it wears off?) and write down what you will do specifically to keep that feeling viable.

12. What mindset will you need to put yourself in to continue this feeling? What must you convince yourself of in order to justify your means to keeping your first-sip feeling alive? Write it all down. Be thorough and specific.

13. Is this who you really are?

14. Who are you really? Who are you before the first hit and the chaotic mind-fudge journey it took you on?

15. Who do you like better, the real you or the person you became after the first hit?

16. What will engaging the first hit cost you?

17. What will not engaging the first hit cost you? Be truthful about the euphoric twenty-minute rewards you're giving up. It's not wrong to want these feelings. Quenching them with your addictive thing, however, may not be your best option for sustaining your quenched craving.

18. Is the cost from your answer to 16 or 17 greater? Either way there's a cost. Life is sucky like that sometimes. Choosing your consequence wisely is your greatest option for feeling alive and satisfying the feelings you crave.

Robert Downy Jr. is said to have stated, "I guess sometimes I want to have a drink with dinner, but then I remember I've got plans for Christmas."

Wanting what you want is not wrong. It is not a flaw. It does not mean you have a problem. Play your want on fast-forward before acting on it, to get what you really want. To show up for your future plans feeling and being alive.

For those of us who need this book, the truth is, we become a different person after the first hit. And that person, not the authentic us, makes poor decisions, lives in their head, and believes the lies of false remedies to what we want. The only real way to stay true to who you are is to not become that person you become after taking the first hit.

Patterns

You don't need to keep doing something just because you did it that way in the past. You can rewire your brain's patterns. Neuroplasticity refers to the lifelong capacity of the brain to change and rewire itself in response to the stimulation of learning and experience. Change is plausible and possible. Just because your family did something a certain way doesn't mean you have to. You get to move past your past if you want to. You get to replace old rituals with new rituals.

So often I have a client declare their pattern to me in the first session: *I am a procrastinator. I suffer from____. I have a drinking problem because it runs in my family. I…* You get what you focus on. You grow into your declarations. Stating that you have a pattern will keep you in that pattern. If you want to think different thoughts, make neuroplasticity work in your favor.

One way to do this is to change your language to, "in the past . . ." before declaring what you want to declare. Or—don't declare it at all. You receive what you speak. You collect the labels you stick on yourself. If you want to disrupt a pattern, dismantle it altogether and don't give it power by speaking of it further. Speak and think about what you want, not what you want to move past. Leave what no longer serves you in the past and declare and believe what you want instead. Nothing worth doing is easy. It took time to establish the pattern you want to dump. It will take time to replace it with a better habit.

> **Nothing worth doing is easy. It took time to establish the pattern you want to dump. It will take time to replace it with a better habit.**

Topping Off

Just because a pattern is not good for one person does not mean it is not good for you. Not all patterns will harm you. I love espresso. When I make one, I hit the button a second time to top off my pour. Always. It's my pattern. Our espresso machine has a special setting for me that Scott programmed to account for the extra ten-second brew. The funny thing is, I top off the custom pour anyway. I do this. My brain does this. When I drank alcohol, I always felt the need to top off my drink. Always. I'm wired for a little extra and I love this part about me. My desire to top off works to my benefit. When I work out, I always do at least two extra reps than the virtual trainer on my app tells me to. It's a beautiful thing that my brain works this way—if it's not alcohol I'm topping off.

Heating Up

Another brain quirk of mine is that I tend to be an all-or-nothing thinker. Our gas fireplace has flame height settings from 1 to 5. In the three years I've lived with the fireplace, I've selected only 1 or 5. Why not 2, 3, or 4? I'm sure they are wonderful heat settings. But I choose all or nothing.

Your brain is as much addicted to your routine as the substance.

What's your thing? What do you need more of? Is that thing moving you forward, is it a moot point, or is it hurting you? An extra dollop of coffee doesn't hinder me as alcohol would, so I don't worry about or analyze why I do it. I let it be.

High, low, or medium heat are neither wrong nor right. The point is to stay aware of the patterns that serve you and those that don't. Your brain is as much addicted to your routine as the substance. Pattern the habits you want to keep and scrap the ones you don't.

Exercise

What is a pattern you notice in yourself that worked to your detriment?

_____

_____

_____

_____

Is it possible you could use this pattern to your benefit?

_____

_____

_____

_____

If not, write it down here so we can focus on dumping it.

_____

_____

_____

_____

If you can use it to your benefit, first accept that your brain is wired in this direction and give yourself a pat on the back. (Literally, stop and pat yourself on the back. Now, please.) Next, list ways you will flip your instinct from harmful to helpful.

_____

_____

_____

_____

Chapter 22

Dopamine Reset

Because we've transformed the world from a place of scarcity to a place of overwhelming abundance: Drugs, food, news, gambling, shopping, gaming, texting, sexting, Facebooking, Instagramming, YouTubing, tweeting . . . the increased numbers, variety and potency of highly rewarding stimuli today is staggering.[29]

—Dr. Anna Lembke, *Dopamine Nation*

Let's revisit the fun we had discussing neurotransmitters. I explained why taking a thirty- to ninety-day break from a vice helps to recalibrate our neural pathways to their natural levels, thus alleviating depression, anxiousness, stress, sleeplessness, and other unwanted effects of manipulating our own brain chemistry.

The "dopamine fast" fad has become popular among wellness enthusiasts and health gurus. What is it? A popular trend circulating on social media called "dopamine detox" involves taking a break from behaviors we turn to for a quick boost—primarily social media, gaming, and TV—to recalibrate our brain's reward pathways.

It's important to address some common misconceptions about the trend. First, the word *detox* describes the removal of something unnatural and harmful. Dopamine is neither. It is also not being removed. The goal is to detox the behavior, not dopamine. One accurate term for this example could be *digital detox*. It is also not a "dopamine fast." When we fast from a behavior such as looking at digital screens, drug use, pleasure or emotional eating, gaming, gambling, shopping, porn, thrill seeking, and recreational drug use, we starve the reward pathway associated with that behavior; however, dopamine is still present in our brain. It is a digital fast, shopping fast, alcohol fast, sugar fast, and so on—not a dopamine fast. The stimulus we want to be less dependent on is what is cut out during the fast, and when it is, our dopamine levels get reset to a natural and healthier state, which changes our pattern of dependence on the addictive thing. The process is a fantastic way to commit to changing a habit.

Another misconception is that during a dopamine recalibration we must cut out all behaviors that bring us pleasure. Doing that could ignite a host of new problems—as well as just plain suck. To recalibrate your dopamine without losing your mind, cut out, or fast from, one unwanted dopamine-specific behavior at a time.

Haley Weiss, a contributor for *TIME*, writes, "Though some evidence suggests that taking a break from certain unhealthy behaviors can prove transformative, most research focuses on clinical addictions, not the daily temptations we all face. That hasn't stopped content creators from overstating the science to promise unmatched happiness, productivity, academic success, and lots of money from a digital detox—all unrealistic claims. It's just a temporary break, and while that can be nice, it won't change your life. Real change takes more active work."[30]

Pulling a Geographic

Knowing it takes around thirty to ninety days to reset brain chemistry to a new pattern raises awareness in areas beyond addiction. When I was a mom of college students, I noticed in the parent groups several first-year students who wanted to move home or transfer to a different school. They were out of their comfort zone, hitting a pain threshold, and tempted to ease the pain by rationalizing a remedy for it. Orientation week usually covers, for parents and students, the importance for first-year college students to stick it out until Thanksgiving before making decisions to leave. They must cleanse the habitualized comforts of home and create healthy new neural pathways. When temptations to throw in the towel before the ninety days are given in to, false notions like, *This school isn't for me, I don't like this town*, or *I made a mistake going to college* may be believed. Before making any physical changes, it is best to give new patterns a chance to take hold.

Shifting physical location to ease, numb, or delay emotional trepidation is also common to people fresh in recovery. But "pulling a geographic" won't heal your discomfort. Allowing newly created patterns to settle in your brain and body will.

> **Recovery is uncovering your authentic self—the parts of you that alcohol, food, busyness, procrastination, changing geographic location, or your habit of choice has masked.**

Recovery is uncovering your authentic self—the parts of you that alcohol, food, busyness, procrastination, changing geographic location, or your habit of choice has masked.

Once you've chosen sobriety, you must sit with discomfort, especially for the first three months of abstinence. Like many hard things worth doing, staying the course will be fruitful. You've taken the mask off and exposed yourself to new emotions and perplexing situations. You're on a roller coaster and it's going up, down, twisty, and turny. You will not get stuck in the upside-down loop. Keep your safety restraint on (your sobriety) and the loop will set you right side up and coast to a comfortable respite. Catch your breath during the respite. The next loop is coming. You are not going to fall out of the coaster. You are safe.

The twists and turns are natural. You get to ride the tracks without soaring off them. Eventually the variety will become familiar and perhaps even a welcome excitement.

Exercise

Here are some coaching questions to move you forward:

1. What do you want—really want?

   Don't want sobriety because it's right. Want sobriety because it's the most exciting way to be you. The best release. The best reward. An abundant sober lifestyle isn't only for people who need it. It's also for people who want it. Being grateful for sobriety will keep you sober. Being resentful of sobriety may keep you relapsing.

2. Why do you want it?

   You can have what you want. If you believe you want to stay in your harmful habit, why do you want that? What will you gain? If you believe you want to abstain from that habit, why do you want to be free? What will you gain? What are the costs of continuing your habit in an attempt to "have it all"? What are the costs of abstaining from that habit in an attempt to have it all?

3. Will you "have it all" by partaking in moderation?

   What will moderation entail? What will moderation cost you? Will you gain even more by abstaining?

Chapter 23

Be a Badass

These aren't the droids you're looking for.[31]
—Obi-Wan Kenobi, *Star Wars*

NY SUBSTANCE THAT IS HARMFUL FOR YOUR mind or body is not the edge you are seeking. You deserve an even edgier, more sustainable thrill. Look, we live comfortably. We crave excitement. Outside substances or harmful behaviors make us feel alive. Until they don't. What else makes you feel alive? Running? Love? Nature? A hobby? Find what moves you to an exciting edge without crushing you.

I get it. You don't want to give up excitement and badassness by giving up your habit—and you don't have to! When you decide to pursue a sober life, be it sober from salt, simple carbs, drugs, alcohol, gambling, or any hindrance to your badassery, you are gaining adventure, not losing it. It may take time (perhaps ninety days) for you to believe this is true. Choose to believe me for now, even if you don't feel like it. If you're convicted that sobriety is a must for you, yet you don't *feel* like committing just yet, then act as if what I say is true, for now, and your feeling will become authentic in time—I promise.

Any substance that is harmful for your mind or body is not the edge you are seeking. You deserve an even edgier, more sustainable thrill.

If alcohol is what you've decided to live free of, then once alcohol clears out, you'll notice other hindrances to living the life you want. Maybe simple carbohydrates and sugar become new hindrances because they change your state of mind. You've used them to stall what you know in your gut you are meant to achieve. You've used them as an excuse to plateau and not get after what you know you're created to get after. Distractions like this work brilliantly as a pause button by distracting your focus to how you just mucked up your system. They take your focus off what lies ahead and keep it stuck in what you just ingested.

Harmful distractions want to hijack your magnificence and put you on pause. There are things in life that will work against you, and that resistance keeps you gritty and growing. What are those things for you? Be aware of them so you can invite the resistance instead of being crushed by it.

Not all distractions are harmful. Be discerning about which distractions are helping you quit a harmful habit and which are thwarting your quitting by substituting one vice for another. To stay vigilant, ask yourself:

- *Is this distraction going to become another harmful habit I'll want to quit in the future?*
- *Is this distraction helping me get through the first thirty to ninety days of quitting the most harmful habit to me?* (For example, many people use chocolate to get through an alcohol detox because alcohol has become an unsafe habit for them, and chocolate is not. They can calibrate their chocolate intake when necessary. Should chocolate be a major problem for that person, a different reward activity is best used as a substitution for the vice they are quitting.)

The great news is, these temporary distractions are not in control. You are smarter and stronger than momentary thoughts, cravings, or temptations. The craving is not there to destroy you. It's there as an opportunity for you to push through and establish a new pattern of power for yourself.

Sometimes I subconsciously entertain cravings to procrastinate what I am meant to do. It's my human nature, so it's not wrong. It's just not the best practice for the life I want. Once I become aware this has happened, I can bring the procrastination to my conscious mind and move forward. When I live free of any state-changing hindrances to living all in, I get to show up and find out what life has in store for me. What's next? Who am I meant to serve? What do I get to do?

For me, eliminating state-changing substances that get me temporarily high is the best way to feel consistently high and alive. I love an edgy feeling. I love feeling excited, alive, and adventurous. It's one reason I drank. It's also why drinking stopped working for me. Life has many authentic adventurous, exciting, and edgy moments available to you. When you quench your desire for aliveness with any state-altering substance, you halt real excitement. You'll squelch true edginess with a cheap fake and deny yourself the real deal.

Let's dive into a few more tips for being extraordinary:

Variety

Embrace the rhythm of variety. We are not meant to trudge forward in one state of mind and body consistently. Every season brings variety and exciting change. Don't force your *shoulds* on yourself. Allowing "shoulds" on yourself may drive you to pick up reckless thoughts or behaviors to satisfy the feeling you denied yourself by not leaning into the cadence of your current season. Allow yourself the rhythm of rest, work, and life. What excites you? What feeling do you love? What state-changing substances stop you from showing up for the life you want—the one you know in your gut you are meant to live?

When you quench your desire for aliveness with any state-altering substance, you halt real excitement. You'll squelch true edginess with a cheap fake and deny yourself the real deal.

Be curious about where you need variety and where you need routine in your life. You may thrive best by creating healthy rituals around the things you can control, like what time you wake up and your exercise schedule, and embracing variety around things you cannot control, like daylight savings, exercising when out of town, and so on. You can have a routine and be flexible when life's agenda changes that routine.

KISS (Keep it Simple, Silly)

Simplicity is a key to keeping mentally fit. Five simple suggestions to mind your mind are:

- Eat clean. Move away from preservatives and fake foods and toward nutrient-dense, whole foods.
- Exercise. Move your body.
- Engage in community and friendships. Don't isolate yourself.

- Spend time outdoors. Enjoy sunshine and nature daily when possible.
- Routine. Stick to structure around attainable rituals that serve you, and embrace variety around your life's realistic agenda.

The goal isn't to study or think yourself into behaviors that serve you. The goal is growing to love what is good for you by choosing invigorating decisions one day at a time. Love what energizes you and stay curious about the things that exhaust you. Harmful habits are a temporary energy boost and an exhausting lifestyle drain. Growth and being worn out don't mix.

To keep things simple, remember the fundamentals. The simplicity of our vision board exercise in chapter 19 did not detract from its impact, because envisioning what you want is a foundational success tool. Pick anyone who's among the best in the world at what they do and look up what they've said about fundamentals. Michael Jordan has been quoted as saying, "Winners don't just learn the fundamentals, they master them. You have to monitor your fundamentals constantly because the only thing that changes will be your attention to them."

To flex the beef of basics, answer these questions rapidly, with the first answer that comes to mind:

1. What is something you are currently very talented or an expert at?
2. Think back to your first experience doing this thing. What is your first memory of learning about this thing that made an impact on how you perform it?

3. Now consider your thing in the present. What is the most impactful thing today to your performance of that same thing?

4. Are your answers to numbers 2 and 3 the same or similar? If so, the most fundamental lesson learned is still the most impactful.

I asked Scott, a talented golfer, these questions. His first impactful lesson, when he was ten years old, came from a video his grandfather had him watch about the physics of his golf swing. The video helped show him instead of telling him what to do. He took a lesson the other day, at age fifty-five, to improve his swing, which he did. I asked what he learned in the lesson that made his swing better. He answered that the lesson included a video reminder of the same fundamental technique he'd learned at age ten. The reminder to monitor his fundamentals was key to placing his attention back on them.

Harmful habits are a temporary energy boost and an exhausting lifestyle drain.

I answered the questions as a mom, since that is what I have my ten-thousand-plus hours at. My first impactful lesson came from the nurse on my first night of motherhood. Helping me feed my son in the hospital that night, as milk squirted everywhere but in the baby's mouth, the nurse said, "You're focused on doing it right. There is no magic to this; it's nature. Try focusing instead on your son." She called it. I was thinking about all the how-to nursing lessons I'd read and how none of them prepared me for the real thing. As soon as I got out of my head and became present in nourishing my child, the feeding worked naturally. It wasn't perfect and there was still a lot of leakage, but he got nourished. That child is twenty-six years old today and the nurse's advice is still fundamentally true. There's no magic to parenting. It's natural. I must focus on my child, not my own ability to parent "right."

Fundamentals are basic and simple. It is up to us to keep our attention on what has worked from the start rather than complicating our process with overthinking, and that is not always easy. Simple does not mean easy.

You Get What You Focus On

Don't think of green. Don't think of green. Don't think of green. What are you thinking about? Green, of course! Here's the deal: Your thought language drives your focus. Your mind will latch like Velcro to your focus—good or bad. Focusing on what you don't want will stick you with that negative mindset.

The words you allow to rule your subconscious matter, and today is the perfect time to refocus your mind. You get what you focus on, so:

- focus on what you want—*not* what you don't want.
- focus on what you can control—*not* what you can't.
- focus on what you have—*not* what's missing.

Simply put, mind your mind space. If a thought is garbage, toss it out to make room for the good stuff. If past gunk starts to suck you down in its quicksand, free your mind by focusing on where you want to go.

The words you allow to play in your head matter—and moving forward is a thinking thing you can control. Peak performance in life and sobriety demands focus. Choose your focus; otherwise, other things, habits, or people will choose for you.

The Four Fs

My Four Fs Framework is a simple way to use your feelings as action signals to spot harmful self-talk.

1. *Feel it.* Stop and get curious when you feel a way you don't want to feel. None of your feelings are wrong; they are just alarm bells to inspire you to become inquisitive instead of cuckoo. So, stop and celebrate your awareness.

2. *Find it.* Next, ask yourself: *What words or thought just went through my mind or out of my mouth?* This led to the feeling.

3. *Fact-check it.* Now, ask yourself, *Is that true? Is this thought or question serving me?*

4. *Frame it.* If it's not moving you in the direction you want to go, frame it to something better. Flip untrue, unhelpful words to positive statements that work in your favor.

Self-Sabotage

Sometimes self-sabotaging, the phenomenon of standing in your own way, is easier than moving ahead. Here is one example of self-sabotaging thoughts: *If I don't feel tip-top, or if I have a ten-pound layer of puff on my body, I must not be meant to do that thing I thought I was created to do.*

Living in a peak state is meant for others, not me. I am typical. I am average. I will stay comfortable with the status quo. Lies! You are meant for magnificence. You are created for community and to serve the world according to your design and mission. You were not created to sit around and brainstorm reasons for not getting up, out, and after it. You are created to feel and to live. You are created to embrace chaos, enjoy calmness, and experience all that exists in the middle.

If you're tempted to self-sabotage:

- Stop and celebrate your awareness (sabotaging thoughts are not harmful, but acting on them will be).
- Revisit your why (remind yourself of the reason you committed to your goal).
- Choose your hard (weigh the cost of working toward your goal vs. the cost of ditching your goal).

One weird thought that tickled my mind during my twenty-three years as a stay-at-home mom was, *If I get to an awesome level of myself and master my peak state, what if I'm disappointed? What if my life circumstances don't match how good I feel and what I'm ready for? What if I feel great and still must stay home, do laundry, grocery shop, cook, drive carpool, and clean?* I was tempted to let my sloth flag fly because I had a limiting belief that feeling great and dressing sharp was for people able to take their greatness outside of the house, into the exciting beyond. I almost self-sabotaged to avoid feeling like I was missing out on whatever I imagined was on the other side of mommyhood. I was scared that if I invested in self-care, I'd be disappointed that it was a waste. Thank goodness I shut down the limiting belief before acting on it. Instead, I decided, so what! It's worth keeping myself in peak physical and mental condition because, no matter my tasks, I want to feel alive while doing them.

The truth is that even mundane tasks are important if they are my lot in life. I reminded myself that raising babies, teens, and young adults is sacred work. My life may not have looked as flashy then as little me dreamed it would. It was exciting, though. And now that the kids are grown and flown, I cannot imagine a more invigorating, purposeful mission to have been on. The energy, love, commitment, and time I poured into the kids is life's greatest reward these days. Watching the three of them thrive and meet their significant others, well, I can't think of anything more thrilling. Staying the course is exciting. Self-sabotage is a beast.

Boredom and Rhythm

The truth is, the high we chase is never as exciting as the feeling we get waking up hungover free—from sugar, alcohol, or other vices. If you feel bored, giving your distraction of choice another shot will not result in the excitement you desire. A hangover is not the excitement you seek. Don't give your habit another chance just because sobriety feels boring. Hangxiety and regret are not the thrills you seek.

Doing scary things can be thrilling in a helpful way. For me, some scary and satisfying substitutes for harmful habits are skiing, trail running, nature, public speaking, and being with animals, especially big animals such as horses.

I love stories too. I used to think enjoying movies and books to escape and jump into the excitement of another person's tale was weak. It's not. It's interesting. Watching the television series *Vampire Diaries* on a snowy day no longer riddles me with guilt and embarrassment. Being hungover from a substance that's harmful for me does. Embrace what excites you and even helps you escape for a bit. A harmless substitute to the fleeting excitement of harmful substances is a sustainable plan for people like you and me, even if your self-help books on excellence preach otherwise.

Choose wisely what works for you. If your habit isn't working for you, be nice to yourself about what you replace it with when necessary.

Keep No Record of Wrongs

As a rigid thinker, I easily fall into the trap of remembering each way I screw up. And when I cannot heap any more record keeping onto my own shoulders, I off-load it to others. I drift seamlessly toward picking on what I believe others' flaws to be. It's gross, so I work to stay aware of it.

First Corinthians 13:5 helps me with this: "It [love] does not dishonor others, it is not self-seeking, it is not easily angered, it keeps no record of wrongs." The NLT version says, "it keeps no record of being wronged." I don't want to keep a record of my own wrongs, other people's wrongs, or the times I believe I was wronged. This verse from Scripture frees me. I'm off the hook for recordkeeping duties (which is not my favorite anyway).

Forgiveness for others comes easier to me than forgiving myself. Forgiving others puts the ball back in my court where I can control it. This is a nifty trick for a people pleaser. As I mentioned in chapter 3, both people pleasing and apologizing when I have nothing to apologize for are means of controlling my feelings. This gets tricky when the forgiveness I seek to feel better is not granted.

Several years ago, a friend was offended at something I said. I didn't mean to cause offense, and I dearly love the person my comment landed on. I felt horrible. I wanted to crawl under a rock and erase the moment from time. I groveled and apologized and asked to discuss further. The friend asked to move on without further discussion. I was denied my chance for forgiveness, the one thing I believed would take the wretched pit in my stomach away. It confused me and I was quite rattled for weeks over the situation. Finally, my mentor firmly said, "Chris, you apologized, and you don't need their forgiveness to feel better. It is your friend's choice not to hear your explanation. They don't want to talk about it and that is their right. You've cleaned your side of the street up, now let them maintain their side how they choose."

I learned that forgiving others does not equal being forgiven. Forgiving myself is a decision only I can make, and waiting on another person's acknowledgment of me is a selfish attempt to control the way I feel. The only thing I have control over is to respect another's right to move on without discussion, then forgive myself. Wanting a pardon is wanting to manipulate the way I feel. The second half of the Prayer of St. Francis of Assisi (popular in recovery groups) reads, "Grant that I may not so much seek to be consoled as to console, to be understood as to understand, to be loved, as to love. For it is in giving that we receive, it is in pardoning that we are pardoned."[32]

Positivity

I alternate living in Los Angeles and Colorado. Currently I'm in LA and I just got over the flu. My brain and body needed a pick-me-up, so I went on a run to feel human. Shuffling along in my fanny pack and sweatshirt I slept in the night before, doing my post-flu best, an athletic specimen of a human ran past, encouraging me with, "You're perfect, you're perfect!" One of the things I love about Southern California is the positivity, creativity, and love of being one's best self.

When framing a circumstance, I'd rather be optimistic and wrong than pessimistic and right.

"Positive psychology" is the formal name for the approach that helps a person develop their strengths instead of attempting to repair their faults. What if instead of seeing yourself as broken, worthless, or damaged, you saw yourself as a whole human who becomes even better by building on existing strengths? You don't need fixing, because you are not broken. That runner's chant, "You're perfect," didn't mean perfect in a high-standard sense. Just the opposite, it meant you're beautiful just as you are.

Positive psychology is not toxic positivity. Toxic positivity places emphasis on only "looking on the bright side." For example, it is using encouraging words ("just think positive") to make a person feel better without validating reality and their real struggles. Positive psychology builds resilience and teaches our brains to see the good in adverse situations while also acknowledging the adversity. When framing a circumstance, I'd rather be optimistic and wrong than pessimistic and right.

Being sober goes against society's current norm. A lifestyle of sobriety is badass. Being in shape is badass. Being positive is badass.

Chapter 24

Boundaries, Parenting, and Friendships

To be yourself in a world that is constantly trying to make you something else is the greatest accomplishment.

—Attributed to Ralph Waldo Emerson

There's a fine line between setting benefi- cial boundaries and loving people well. As a sensitive person, I feel terrible when someone else feels terrible. Does that make their feelings my responsibility? No. For me to manage this, I acknowledge the other person's feelings (to myself) and give myself a firm reminder that their feelings are their business. Preferably, I do this before mucking up the situation by jumping in, bombarding them with my own selfish concern, and attempting to fix.

Although throwing myself at that person with gushing concern may appear kind, thoughtful, and the sign of a good friend, it's not. I would only be "fixing" to make myself feel better. I feel bad when others feel bad, so attempts to control another person's feelings are an attempt at manipulating my own feelings.

Allowing people the freedom to behave and feel however they want is the way to have authentic relation- ships with fellow humans. If I feel sad when another is sad, or angry when I perceive a person is not behaving as I expected them to, that is my business, not theirs. Remember that unmet expectations often result in anger. For me to make another person's feelings my business is more about me than it is my concern for them.

Your personal boundaries are your responsibility, not others' responsibility. Setting boundaries is about being accountable to your own wellness, not holding another person accountable to your mental health. You cannot control others, only yourself. You cannot set expectations for other people.

As a good friend, I can listen to what they want and need from me. It is OK to jump in when what they need is an invitation to me. It is not OK for me to jump in uninvited as an attempt to quell my own discomfort.

In parenting this looks like allowing kids to feel disappointed without trying to fix things. Life is unfair, and if I constantly lean in to remedy my child's discomfort, I am only remedying my own and in fact being a hindrance to my child's growth.

Where this gets tricky is when protecting my energy or personal boundary risks disappointing another person. Since other people's disappointments become my own, I must stay vigilant in my personal commitments and remember feeling crummy does not make respecting my personal boundary wrong. I cannot please every person in my sphere and also have energy left to serve those I am meant to serve.

My close friends are the ones who energize me, and my time with them is precious. These are my safe people. The ones who extend grace when I'm at my ugliest. The ones with whom I can vomit my fleshiness to. The ones who gently remind me it's OK to be human then also remind me I'm better than my flaws. They set me back on my growth track and keep the train moving forward. They are brave, bold, authentic, and full of grace.

So where is that line between protecting a life-giving circle of trust and being a cliquey mean girl? There's no magic formula. You can't make everyone happy. You are

> **Life is unfair, and if I constantly lean in to remedy my child's discomfort, I am only remedying my own and in fact being a hindrance to my child's growth.**

not responsible for people's feelings. You do not have the power to manipulate the desires and satisfaction of another person. If your goal is to be kind and polite to others, you'll pull this off best by sticking to your personal boundaries, protecting your energy, and cherishing what fills your cup.

And remember, you have control over the boundaries you set, not whether others respect them. If another person is disappointed that they do not get more of your time, that is their right to work out, not yours. When you believe the lie that you can satisfy everyone, you'll be tempted to meddle, and the meddling and manipulating will create resentment toward the person you set out to appease. In the end, you would have come closest to being kind and polite by sticking to what and who you are responsible for—yourself.

Do not mistake what you can control (yourself) for what you wish you could control (other people's feelings) to make yourself feel better. Let's revisit the first few lines of the serenity prayer:

> *God, grant me the serenity to accept*
> *The things I cannot change,*
> *The courage to change the things I can,*
> *And the wisdom to know the difference.*

By sitting with your own discomfort over another person's disappointment, you are respecting them and lovingly creating space for them to grow.

Chapter 25

Celebrate

A calm and modest life brings more happiness than the pursuit of success combined with constant restlessness.

—Attributed to Albert Einstein

I BELIEVE WE GET WHAT WE FOCUS ON. WHEN I WAS attempting to moderate alcohol, my limiting story became, *Not drinking is causing me to focus on drinking. If I just drink one, I'll stop focusing on it.* And, *Aren't all these sobriety meetings, where we talk about drinking, causing me to focus even more on the very thing I want to stop thinking about?* While the logic isn't insane, it's no surprise it doesn't hold up.

I've learned that what works for me to stay supported while not focusing on drinking is to focus on what I want instead. I focus on how vibrant my alcohol-free life is. I celebrate it. I do celebrate my sober milestones because it makes me happy. I am careful to celebrate my soberversaries as another year of freedom instead of another year of not drinking. This keeps my focus on what works instead of what hasn't worked in the past. I know many people who don't count their alcohol-free days, months, or years and choose not to celebrate milestones. That's great because

I am careful to celebrate my soberversaries as another year of freedom instead of another year of not drinking.

that's what works for them. What counts is that you're celebrating yourself today. While we all share different stories, different "day ones," and different amounts of continuous sobriety, we all share this moment. I celebrate sober timelines because that works for me now. Focus on what you want. Celebrate what you've gained, not what you're giving up.

I don't have ___ days. I have thirteen years and ___ days. For me, the disappointment of starting over needed to be ditched. Starting over at day one doesn't erase the work I did previously. If recovery is recovering one's true self, then I had already recovered her. She was still safe. I will never stop evolving. Don't let perfectionism, pride, or ego get in the way of accepting a new day one or trick you into believing you must keep a day counter. Get curious about what works best for you to celebrate your success and evolve with changes that work even better over time.

> **Don't let perfectionism, pride, or ego get in the way of accepting a new day one or trick you into believing you must keep a day counter.**

Stay Excited

Somewhere after year ten I stopped thinking about sobriety. Stopped working for it. It was easy and as natural as not needing to work at being a female. It just was who I was. So I stopped attending support groups. When people asked me how many years I'd been sober, they got excited about my answer, cheering, "Way to go, that's amazing!" It didn't feel amazing at that point. It felt as amazing as someone saying good job for tying my shoe. I now know that was part of the problem. I remember how excited I was when my kids each learned to tie their shoes. It was a huge whoop-and-holler celebration. Not when they were ten years old, though. I realized I was treating my sobriety like an expected child development phase that most humans can master. It's not. My sobriety was a miracle, and I had let the magic wear off.

Sobriety is ambitious. It is nothing less than miraculous and deserves awe. It isn't only the absence of your habit. It requires a sober mind, honesty, and commitment. It demands confronting and accepting every reason you chose your habit over feeling and facing your emotions and circumstances. It deserves celebration. I had allowed myself to forget that.

I was treating my sobriety like an expected child development phase that most humans can master. It's not. My sobriety was a miracle, and I had let the magic wear off.

Celebrating my sobriety was something that had been my favorite thing to do in the early years. I loved chip meetings. I loved counting my months and years and celebrating the heck out of them. Then I lost touch with my sober community and started looking at the differences instead of the similarities. The greatest similarity to me and others in sobriety is that we all have today. Sure, I have a lot of years of continuous sobriety, and I do celebrate that now. I would not be who I am or where I am without my recovery. However, my length of sobriety does not make me less susceptible than the next person to picking up a drink. No matter how much time any sober person has, we all must celebrate that we stayed sober today.

Exercise

Like the vision board, the verbal affirmation is a foundational tool that works. Remember the *Saturday Night Live* character Stuart Smalley who coached viewers to look in the mirror and recite, "I'm good enough, I'm smart enough, and doggone it, people like me!" The hilarious daily affirmations skit made light of the fundamental self-help tool, but as hilarious as the skit was, affirmations are no joke. They work!

Affirmations train your brain to trust what you say to yourself and change your neuroplasticity to create brain patterns that serve you and remove those that don't. The more emotion and motion (physical) you invest in your affirmations, the faster and farther they will take you. Like most things worth working for, affirmations require repetition and conditioning. Be patient as they take hold and become part of your physiology and nervous system. They will take hold, and with conditioning over time will become your new second nature. This is what mastery looks like. The higher the intention (motion and emotion), the more impact will be made. Simple, not easy!

Reflect on the person you want to become (from chapter 4), your new beliefs (from chapter 5), your commitments (from chapter 8), and your future letter (from chapter 17) and turn them into a set of affirmations using present tense and positive language. For example, use *and* instead of *but*; *I am* instead of *I will*; *I choose* instead of *I don't*; and *I get to* instead of *I have to*. If I had been coaching Stuart Smalley, I would have had him drop the "enough" so the affirmation read, "I'm good, I'm smart, and I like me." I know you will come up with even heartier affirmations for yourself than Smalley did. Now, let's get to it.

Using the answers from the preceding paragraph, create affirmations for yourself. Stick to about three to eight words per affirmation. Start each with the following suggested words:

- I am _____(who you want to become).
- I believe _____(your new story/belief).
- I choose to _____(your commitment).
- I'm grateful that I now know _____ (taken from letter to future self).
- I get to _____.

Now that you have some starter affirmations written down, practice repeating them with intention. Condition them into your physiology and create new neural pathways. Decide for each:

- What is the emotion of the affirmation?
- What is the motion of the affirmation?
- How will I condition this truth for myself even further?

Here are some tips for making affirmations stick:

- Write them on sticky notes and place them where you'll see them several times daily.
- Recite to yourself in the mirror.
- Use different pitch, tone, and volume when reciting. The sillier, the better.

- Use hand and body motions when reciting. Jump up and down. Spin around. Again, be silly. You are scrambling old patterns and building new ones.
- Take a picture of your written affirmation and use it as your smartphone wallpaper.
- Record yourself reciting your affirmation and watch the recording upon waking and before bed.
- What else? Capture impactful ideas for yourself to turn affirmations into reality.

Chapter 26

There's No Place like Home

What I've discovered is that the human potential is limitless, and I've seen the impossible achieved over and over again.
—JIMMY CHIN, *EDGE OF THE UNKNOWN*

TRUSTING THE WOMAN AT MY VERY FIRST SUPPORT meeting, that I am not a monster, continues to be the most impactful pivot point to my self-belief. Her words to me—"It is not your fault. You are alcoholic. It is like an allergy. You never have to have another drink again."— still fuel me to believe I am worthy regardless of my past, present, or future behaviors or thoughts—and you are worthy as well. You don't earn worthiness; you are born with it.

The memorable words of the Good Witch from *The Wizard of Oz*, "Never let those ruby slippers off your feet for a moment, or you will be at the mercy of the Wicked Witch of the West!" can be a dynamic metaphor for self-worth. The story's plot is based on getting Dorothy's magic ruby slippers off her feet. The Wicked Witch, however, was unable to take Dorothy's shoes and got zapped when she tried. The only way the slippers could be removed from Dorothy's feet was if Dorothy decided to take them off herself. Glinda, the Good Witch of the North, gave Dorothy the directions to finally get her home: "You've always had the power, my dear, you just had to learn it for yourself. Tap the heels of your red shoes together three times. Close your eyes and say, 'There's no place like home!'"[33]

Like Dorothy's ruby slippers, regardless of the path you take, your self-worth is a constant. The world and your own (subconscious or conscious) thoughts may

> **Choosing to break free of your stronghold will make your life more fun; however, it cannot make you more valuable than you already are at this moment.**

attempt to take your ruby red slippers—your worth. And just like the Wicked Witch, those attempts to steal, kill, and destroy will be zapped—because your worth and God's grace on you cannot be thwarted. Your value is a constant. God's grace is constant. You are worthy if you're addicted—and you're worthy if you're not. You are under grace if you're addicted—and under grace if you're not. Choosing to break free of your stronghold will make your life more fun; however, it cannot make you more valuable than you already are at this moment.

I want you to choose freedom instead of addiction, because you are worthy of it—not in order to be worthy. You do not need to get clean before taking a bath, and you do not need to learn to love yourself before getting sober. You can get sober now, exactly as you are, because you are loved exactly as you are. That is grace—unmerited favor that cannot be earned. Grace and worthiness are shining on you now, and you cannot thwart them. Attempts to control what you deserve are fruitless. The world cannot take your ruby slippers off, no matter how scuffed and scarred they get. You are not in charge of calcu-

You can get sober now, exactly as you are, because you are loved exactly as you are.

lating your worth, and you do not get to decide whether or not your Creator shines grace on you. Grace is yours to embrace the moment you set down your illusion of control over your own worth. You get freedom. You get to bask in the warmth of grace. You get to tap your heels three times and say, "There's no place like home."

Close your eyes and picture yourself in a new emotional home, soaking in the warm light of grace. Sit in that image and embrace grace until you feel its warmth.

Then, seeing yourself as the valuable, bright light you are, radiate that light out of your body. Every beam is a ray of worth and value. Condition this visualization daily.

Grace is yours to embrace the moment you set down your illusion of control over your own worth.

Now, go shine and show up for the sober life you desire!

Acknowledgments

Huge thanks to:

Scott—for being you. And for loving me no matter what. You are the face of grace in this world, and I am the luckiest to get to spend eternity with you!

Nick, Chloé, Jake, Ruth, and Josh—for your hearts. You are the funniest and most exciting people I've ever had the privilege to hang out with. Your compassion, grit, diligence, and character inspire and impress me more each day. Thank you for your grace, patience, and love.

Jackie and Larry—for being tireless parents. And Jackie, for reading my rough draft and not freaking out.

The best sponsors in the world, Peggy Z. and Donna B.—I have the recovery story I have because of your wisdom, time, grace, and mentorship. Your examples of unselfish leadership taught me what service done with authenticity and humility looks like.

Dana and Steve Clifford—for being my advocates, cheerleaders, mentors, and friends.

Lisa and Mark Averill—for being part of my family's story all these years.

Devon, Rebecca, Melinda, Dana S., Lisa, Dana C., Beth, Lindy, Cindy, Paula, and the women in my front row—It's a privilege to be in yours. I love doing life with you.

Rory and AJ Vaden, Brand Builders Group, and Mission Driven Press—thank you for creating a company rooted in truth and integrity, and for trusting me as a mission-driven messenger. You are a bright light. Keep shining!

Jay Twining—my stellar strategist and coach. Thank you for helping me with *every* thing!

Jeff Mohs—for your hours and energy ensuring this book was go for launch!

Brandon Judd—for your cleverness and insight.

Forefront Books—Becky Philpott, Jennifer Gingerich, Billie Brownell, Justin Batt, and Lauren Ward. You make writing fun!

My friends at the Castle Rock Clubhouse in Colorado—for your ears, presence, attention, and acceptance. You model the meaning of *Grace Yourself*!

Endnotes

1 C. S. Lewis, *The Problem of Pain* (New York: HarperCollins, 2001), 88–89.

2 Lisa Marie Presley, in Harry Nelson, *The United States of Opioids: A Prescription for Liberating a Nation in Pain* (Charleston, SC: Forbes Books, 2019), foreword.

3 Elias Leight, "Gen Z Is Drinking Less and Clubs Aren't Thrilled," *Billboard*, June 6, 2023, https://www.billboard.com/pro /gen-z-drinking-less-bad-club-business/.

4 Katherine Morgan Schafler, *The Perfectionist's Guide to Losing Control* (New York: Penguin Random House, 2023), 2.

5 Schafler. *The Perfectionist's Guide to Losing Control*, 30.

6 Craig Groeschel (@craiggroeschel), "Comparison will either make you feel superior or inferior," Instagram, May 24, 2021, https:// www.instagram.com/craiggroeschel/p/CKorR4zAHQw/.

7 Mel Robbins (@melrobbins), "Saying I'm Sorry," Instagram, November 14, 2021, https://www.instagram.com/p/CWRjvDit_ to/?igsh=MXR5azV0OTZjaTAzOQ%3D%3D&img_index=1.

8 Reinhold Niebuhr, Serenity Prayer.

9 *Merriam-Webster*, s.v. "sober (*adj.*)," accessed July 6, 2024, https://

www.merriam-webster.com/dictionary/sober.

10 These exercise questions are from my book *Living All In*, chapter 8.

11 Viktor Frankl, *Man's Search for Meaning* (Boston: Beacon Press, 1959), 66.

12 Chris Janssen, *Living All In: How to Show Up for the Life You Want* (Colorado: Chris Janssen Coaching LLC, 2022), 26–28.

13 "Frequently Asked Questions: What Is DSM and Why Is It Important?," American Psychiatric Association (APA), accessed July 6, 2024, https://www.psychiatry.org/psychiatrists/practice/dsm/frequently-asked-questions.

14 You can read more about the DSM on the APA's website: https://www.psychiatry.org.

15 *The Holdovers*, directed by Alexander Payne (Miramax, 2024), 1:30.

16 DISC Assessment, https://www.discprofile.com/what-is-disc.

17 CliftonStrengths, Gallup, accessed July 6, 2024, https://www.gallup.com/cliftonstrengths/en/252137/home.aspx.

18 *Twelve Steps and Twelve Traditions*, 78th printing, Alcoholics Anonymous (New York: Alcoholics Anonymous World Services, 2013), 45.

19 *The West Wing*, season 2, episode 10, aired December 19, 2000.

20 *Jane*, National Geographic Documentary Films, 2024, 1:23.

21 Jane Goodall, Jane Goodall Institute, accessed July 7, 2024, https://janegoodall.org/our-story/about-jane/.

22 *The Big Book of Alcoholics Anonymous, Fourth Edition*. Chapter 5, "How It Works," 58–59.

23 *1923*, season 1, episode 3, "The War Has Come Home,"Paramount Plus, written by Taylor Sheridan, 2023.

24 "The War Has Come Home."

25 Jim Gaffigan, *"I'm Too Lazy,"* YouTube, December 2, 2022, Original airdate July 12, 2000, https://www.youtube.com/watch?v=NaACTpYah1w.

26 *Twelve Steps and Twelve Traditions* (New York: Alcoholics Anonymous World Services, 2013), 47.

27 Popular recovery quote. Author anonymous.

28 Alex Honnold, *Edge of the Unknown with Jimmy Chin*, season 1,

episode 1 "The No Fall Zone," 2022.

29 Anna Lembke, MD. *Dopamine Nation* (New York: Dutton, an imprint of Penguin Random House, 2021), 1.

30 Haley Weiss, "The 'Dopamine Detox' Is Having a Moment," *TIME*, June 2, 2023, https://time.com/6284428/does-dopamine-detox-work/.

31 *Star Wars: A New Hope*, directed and written by George Lucas, Lucasfilm, 1977.

32 "Prayer of St. Francis," Science of Mind Spiritual Center, accessed July 8, 2024, https://somspiritualcenterla.org/prayer-of-st-francis?gad_source=1&gclid=CjwKCAjwnK60BhA9Ei-wAmpHZwmGy4BEq59zEj2SqVppjrGJibYZeqR4RyKQSpA8LH-vss1CQRkKcVBoCmLgQAvD_BwE.

33 *The Wizard of Oz*, directed by Victor Fleming, Sony Pictures Studios, 1939.

Notes & Nuggets

NOTES & NUGGETS

NOTES & NUGGETS

NOTES & NUGGETS